Managing for Tomorrow

Global Change and Local Futures

Managing for Tomorrow
Global Change and Local Futures

Edited by
Amy Cohen Paul

PRACTICAL MANAGEMENT SERIES
Barbara H. Moore, Editor

Managing for Tomorrow
Capital Financing Strategies for Local Governments
Capital Projects
Creative Personnel Practices
Current Issues in Leisure Services
The Entrepreneur in Local Government
Ethical Insight, Ethical Action
Hazardous Materials, Hazardous Waste
Human Services on a Limited Budget
Long-Term Financial Planning
Managing New Technologies
Pay and Benefits
Performance Evaluation
Personnel Practices for the '90s
Police Management Today
Police Practice in the '90s
Practical Financial Management
Productivity Improvement Techniques
Risk Management Today
Shaping the Local Economy
Successful Negotiating in Local Government
Telecommunications for Local Government

The Practical Management Series is devoted to the
presentation of information and ideas from diverse
sources. The views expressed in this book are those of
the contributors and are not necessarily those of ICMA.

Library of Congress Cataloging-in-Publication Data

Managing for tomorrow : global change and local futures / edited by
    Amy Cohen Paul.
        p.   cm. — (Practical management series)
    Includes bibliographical references.
    ISBN 0-87326-061-9
    1. Local government.   2. Forecasting.   I. Paul, Amy Cohen.
II. Series.
JS91.M28   1990   90-44792
352—dc20   CIP

Printed in the United States of America.
959493929190
54321

Managing for Tomorrow:
Global Change and
Local Futures

The International City Management Association is the professional and educational organization for chief appointed management executives in local government. The purposes of ICMA are to enhance the quality of local government and to nurture and assist professional local government administrators in the United States and other countries. In furtherance of its mission, ICMA develops and disseminates new approaches to management through training programs, information services, and publications.

Managers, carrying a wide range of titles, serve cities, towns, counties, councils of governments, and state/provincial associations of local governments in all parts of the United States and Canada. These managers serve at the direction of elected councils and governing boards. ICMA serves these managers and local governments through many programs that aim at improving the manager's professional competence and strengthening the quality of all local governments.

The International City Management Association was founded in 1914; adopted its City Management Code of Ethics in 1924; and established its Institute for Training in Municipal Administration in 1934. The Institute, in turn, provided the basis for the Municipal Management Series, generally termed the "ICMA Green Books."

ICMA's interests and activities include public management education; standards of ethics for members; the *Municipal Year Book* and other data services; urban research; and newsletters, a monthly magazine, *Public Management*, and other publications. ICMA's efforts for the improvement of local government management—as represented by this book—are offered for all local governments and educational institutions.

Foreword

"Urban administrators as futurists are responsible for anticipatory management." In 1979, ICMA's *The Essential Community: Local Government in the Year 2000* opened with those words, and local government managers nationwide still subscribe to them.

Our only hope of shaping the future begins with trying to understand it. ICMA's first institutional effort to explore the future was undertaken in 1978 by the Committee on Future Horizons of the Profession. Ten years later, ICMA launched the FutureVisions Consortium, a group of sixty-five local government managers who came together to identify developments likely to affect local government and develop strategies for coping with them.

This volume is, in part, an outcome of the work of the Future-Visions Consortium. It focuses on areas that the consortium has identified as critical to local governments in the coming decades—demographics, economic globalization, technology and information management, human capital and resources, public service, and governance. Like other current "futuring" efforts, the articles in this volume are careful and judicious studies of current trends, analyzed from perspectives that range from the globe to the neighborhood. But whatever the perspective, two common threads unite all the selections: first, that we can and should study the future; and second, that by applying what we learn to the practice of anticipatory management, we can shape a better world.

This book is part of ICMA's Practical Management Series, which is devoted to serving local officials' needs for timely information on current issues and problems.

We wish to extend special thanks to the members of the FutureVisions Consortium, who contributed valuable suggestions on coverage. We are also grateful to Amy Cohen Paul for her work in compiling the volume, to Sandy Chizinsky Leas for her editorial guidance, and to the individuals and organizations that granted ICMA permission to reprint their material. Finally, we wish to thank Mike Freeman, assistant director of the FutureVisions Consortium, for his work obtaining permissions to reprint.

William H. Hansell, Jr.
Executive Director
ICMA

About the Editor

Amy Cohen Paul is president of The Communications Group, Erie, Pennsylvania. Ms. Paul assists local governments and nonprofit organizations with strategic planning projects. As director of the ICMA FutureVisions Consortium, which began in 1988, Ms. Paul worked with sixty-five local government managers to explore major future trends and their implications for local government. Before becoming president of The Communications Group, Ms. Paul was a project director at ICMA. She holds a bachelor's degree in public communication and a master's degree in public administration from The American University.

About the Authors

Unless otherwise noted, the following are the affiliations of the contributors at the time of writing.

Roy Amara, President, Institute for the Future, Menlo Park, California.

Lynda M. Applegate, assistant professor, Harvard Business School.

Jim Braham, staff reporter, *Industry Week.*

James I. Cash, Jr., professor of control, Harvard Business School.

Marvin J. Cetron, president, Forecasting International, Ltd., Arlington, Virginia.

Marj Charlier, staff reporter, *The Wall Street Journal*, Dallas bureau.

Harlan Cleveland, professor emeritus and former dean, Hubert H. Humphrey Institute of Public Affairs, University of Minnesota.

Peter Drucker, writer, consultant, and educator in the field of management sciences.

Brian Dumaine, staff writer, *Fortune* magazine.

Lindsey Grant, retired U.S. foreign service officer; former member, National Security Council staff; and former member, policy planning staff, Department of State.

Jeffrey Hallett, principal, The Present Futures Group, Alexandria, Virginia (current affiliation).

Rosabeth Moss Kanter, Class of 1960 Professor of Business Administration, Harvard Business School.

Norman R. King, city manager, Palm Springs, California.

Frances Moore Lappé, co-convener, Project Public Life.

John L. McKnight, associate director, Center for Urban Affairs and Policy Research, Northwestern University.

D. Quinn Mills, Albert J. Weatherhead, Jr., Professor of Business Administration, Harvard Business School.

Chester A. Newland, professor, School of Public Administration, University of Southern California.

Anthony Newstead, Graduate School of Management, Public Sector Management Institute, Monash University, Melbourne, Australia.

Robert B. Reich, senior editor, *The New Republic.*

Jane F. Roberts, assistant director of communications, U.S. Advisory Commission on Intergovernmental Relations.

Contents

Introduction

Amy Cohen Paul

The time is past for simply reacting to events. Elected and appointed local government officials must work hand in hand with citizens to confront the future with forethought and vision. Those who are not out in front—planning, evaluating new ideas and techniques, and leading change within the organization and the community—are giving up the invaluable opportunity to have a say in tomorrow.

This is not to say that the only successful local governments are being run by futurists: but definite advantages accrue to local government officials who monitor and evaluate future trends in their own organizations, the community, the region, the nation, and the world.

"Futuring" at its best engages a wide cross-section of the community—including not only traditional "positional" leaders such as school superintendents, hospital administrators, and chamber of commerce executives, but also those not typically in leadership positions: disenfranchised residents, elderly and disabled citizens, and school children. Only through broad participation can a community create a strong vision for the future.

The selections included in this volume have one common premise: we can shape our destiny. Although many of the articles are based on trends and experiences in the private sector, they have been chosen for their applicability to the local government environment.

Thinking about the future:
Not just for experts anymore

Demonstrable practical value is the primary reason for the growth of the "futuring" profession. Gloom and doom predictions continue

xvi   Managing For Tomorrow

to lose ground to a more positive approach that stresses action. Harlan Cleveland, author of the first article in the volume, notes that "peering into the future is thus accepted, unassailable in its purpose if not in its multiple models of analysis."

The two articles in the first section share the perspective that forecasting, planning, and thinking about the future are important and desirable. In "The Future of Futurists: What Matters and What Works," Cleveland places futures studies in a global context, delineating dangers and opportunities for humans worldwide. Roy Amara's "Ten Do's and Don'ts of Forecasting and Planning" provides practical advice on forecasting and planning as well as guidelines for integrating planning and action.

Critical connections:
The global economy, society, and education

Our society's future is increasingly driven by economic trends, and our economic future is inextricably linked to education and training. In "As the World Turns," Robert B. Reich contends that the global economy has caused three distinct categories of workers to emerge in America—two of which hold "relatively weak positions in an increasingly global labor market." In Reich's view, education is one of the answers: we must educate our youth to assume a strong position in the global economy. Reich also writes persuasively of the need for the "fortunate fifth"—the group with forty percent of the nation's income—to finance education and health care for the working poor and their children.

In "The Futures That Have Already Happened," Peter Drucker addresses other ways in which global changes will affect our future, focusing on five areas that will be vastly different in the coming years. One in particular has important implications for local government: increasing alliances among nontraditional partners, including local governments, universities, and health-care institutions.

Some nations—Japan among them—are pursuing economic superpower status by striving for technological superiority. According to Anthony Newstead, author of "Future Information Cities: Japan's Vision," Japan has linked its economic policy to dominance in knowledge-based industries. In the proposed "information city" of Kawasaki, the neighborhood office concept would make it possible to use technology not only for work, but also for leisure and to obtain informal education. Perhaps most compelling is the notion of technological links between citizens and local government.

In this time of explosive changes, how can we educate and train workers to compete in the global marketplace? Overwhelmingly, education is the answer, but the specifics of "how to" are far less certain. The last three articles in the section offer several approaches.

In "Class of 2000: The Good News and the Bad News," Marvin J. Cetron focuses on the traditional educational system, citing shocking evidence of the lack of basic reading and math skills among Americans. Cetron warns that both conventional and vocational education are essential to maintaining a competitive workforce, then offers "embarrassingly simple" suggestions for strengthening our schools—such as decreasing class size, lengthening the school year, and using computers more widely.

Cetron's suggestions are aimed at improving the skills of the children now making their way through the educational system—but what of those whom the system has, in effect, already left behind? Employers nationwide are finding that in many cases, literate, job-ready applicants are *made*, not hired. In "Back to Basics," Marj Charlier describes private-sector remediation programs that are designed to ensure that employees have the basic skills necessary to perform their jobs.

In "Training and Education: The Competitive Edge," Jeffrey Hallett agrees that important changes must be made in our educational system, but he is concerned about the form of our national response. "'Back to basics' is a terrible theme and strategy. We need to go forward. . . . This means that we have to be prepared to change everything about education and training." Hallett provides specific suggestions, including an "ageless" training and education system that is responsive to the rapid development of information.

Whatever the approach to improving education and training, the challenge for local governments will be to maintain adequate funding in these areas. Although a skilled workforce is not a luxury but a necessity, local government training programs have traditionally been vulnerable to budget cuts. As the articles in this section make clear, an undereducated, undertrained workforce has serious implications for America's future.

Managing today for the future

If column inches in periodicals indicate the popularity of a topic—or the severity of a problem—then managing for the future is on many people's minds. Both local government managers and corporate CEOs are eager for guidance.

One of the most important ingredients in successful management for the future is really an old idea: leadership from the top. This is among the approaches recommended by Brian Dumaine in "Creating a New Company Culture"; Dumaine warns, however, that the CEO's role is to *guide* change—not to demand it. Dumaine also cautions that the CEO must act, not just talk, and that even the best efforts will yield gradual results—five to ten years "for a significant, organization-wide improvement."

One aspect of both corporate and government culture that is certainly changing—with or without leadership from the top—is the composition of the workforce. In "No, You Don't Manage Everyone the Same," Jim Braham notes that successful organizations will increasingly be those that learn to benefit from diversity. He provides straight talk from corporate leaders whose job is to confront stereotypes and cultural differences head on.

As organizations strive for the level of efficiency and service that will enable them to be competitive in a global marketplace, their configurations have changed. There is less bureaucracy, less hierarchy, and more participation in decision making and problem solving. But such structural changes are often accompanied by dramatic shifts in formal reporting relationships and patterns of organizational power. In "The New Managerial Work," Rosabeth Moss Kanter suggests that the new, more fluid structures imply "very different ways of obtaining and using power." Kanter explains why such changes are likely to confuse managers at first and offers practical suggestions for success in the new, more fluid organizational environment.

One of the ingredients that has contributed to the changing shape of organizations—and that will continue to do so—is technology. In "Information Technology and Tomorrow's Manager," Lynda M. Applegate, James I. Cash, Jr., and D. Quinn Mills paint an exciting vision of a future in which managers "will be able to make their organizations far more responsive than they are today." Applegate, Cash, and Mills caution, however, that managers must "begin thinking about the kind of organization [they] want and taking the steps necessary to prepare for it."

Governance: What's next?

The concluding section of the book brings the future patterns of management even closer to home by looking at governance—from the federal to the neighborhood level. How can governing organizations best respond to emerging needs? What new forms or mechanisms of governance might develop in response to future changes?

In "Foresight: Addressing Tomorrow's Problems Today," Lindsey Grant stresses that comprehensive planning for the future must become an integral part of decision making. In Grant's view, such foresight can be particularly helpful in keeping policymakers focused on "the consequences of policies rather than on emotional responses or preconceptions." Although much of Grant's article focuses on the federal government, many of his suggestions are applicable to local government as well. "Foresight calls for a new approach to thinking, a recognition that things are interconnected, not just conceptually, but vitally."

According to Jane F. Roberts in "Prospects for State-Local Relations," there are signs that state and local governments are beginning to cooperate effectively in "a broad range of entrepreneurial activities and are demonstrating progress in forging state-local partnerships." Roberts describes accomplishments that have resulted from such partnerships and concludes that there is reason for optimism.

Along with state-local partnerships, regional partnerships will become increasingly important in the future. Many issues confronting local governments will require regional solutions: it's not as if air pollution simply stops at a country or a state line. At the October 1989 meeting of the National Civic League, the league's board of directors adopted a statement advocating metropolitan governance: "The successful regions of the next century will be those which learn to think of their entire metropolitan area as their community and take timely action to mobilize joint resources . . . on a metropolitan-wide basis."

Another strategy that can be expected to assume increasing importance in service provision is that advocated by Norman R. King in "Managing the Demand for Government Services." In King's view, government at every level has tended to deal with services from "the supply side": where will we get the necessary resources to increase service levels? King advocates approaching services from the standpoint of demand: how can we, through effective pricing policy, help citizens decide how to allocate *their* resources? King believes that local governments must begin by educating citizens about the true costs of providing services and offers provocative recommendations applicable to a wide range of local and national problems.

Grant, Roberts, the National Civic League, and King have specific recommendations about how to improve governance from the federal to the municipal level. But is there a particular *form* of local governance that holds the greatest promise for the years ahead? Chester A. Newland believes there is. In "The Future of Council-Manager Government," Newland begins his consideration of the future by looking back to ICMA's Committee on Future Horizons of the Profession, which convened in 1978 to explore local government as it might be in the year 2000. Newland then offers a review of the origins and development of council-manager government, concluding that

council-manager government remains the strongest institutional force of transformational politics in practice in the United States. Its basic tenet of collaborative, community-oriented politics, combined with the qualities of disciplined institutions and professionally responsible expertise, stand in contrast to more visible trends in national politics and government.

The two concluding articles in the volume turn from the management and structure of government toward broader issues of political participation and community identity. In "Politics for a Troubled Planet," Frances Moore Lappé offers suggestions for helping to rebuild and renew democracy from the ground up. Lappé describes Project Public Life, which is directed at helping "reformulate the discussion about what 'politics' means in America, in large part through projects that enhance citizen capacity for public judgment and public agency."

The last selection, John L. McKnight's "Regenerating Community," continues the theme of community from a somewhat different perspective. In his provocative article, McKnight contrasts institutions and their programs with people and their communities, concluding that institutions "organize a large group of people so that a few of them will be able to control the rest of them." McKnight celebrates our ability to rise above institutions and create associations: "associations and the community they create are the forum within which citizenship can be expressed. To exclude from our problem-solving capacities the social tool of community is to have taken the heart out of America." McKnight's piece is a fitting conclusion to the book. What is the future of local government, if not a continuing effort to nourish community?

PART 1

Thinking about the Future: Not Just for Experts Anymore

The Future of Futurists: What Matters and What Works

Harlan Cleveland

Will success spoil futures studies?

The success is undeniable. Studying the future is no longer a far-out, fringe activity. It is widely and reputably practiced in corporations, government agencies, universities, think-tanks, and thriving consultancies.

But since the future has not happened yet, what is studied is the subjective product of the human imagination. And it seems to be easier, more fun and more profitable to imagine bad news than good news. For anyone who tries to foresee what might happen, the greatest temptation is to predict catastrophe. It makes headlines, sells books, funds lectures and air travel to distant conferences. If she were living today, Cassandra could not be ignored by order of Apollo; she would be a syndicated columnist and a sought-after consultant.

My question: Is there something about futures studies that inherently requires lugubrious comparisons in which the future turns out to be less desirable than the present? And if there is, won't the future of futurists turn out to be lugubrious too?

Futures studies: a recent phenomenon

It is hard now to remember that the systematic study of the future is so recent a breakthrough in the long history of the art of thinking.

All around us the metaphor of year 2000—and, latterly, more safely distant goal-lines (2010, 2025)—has become a popular framework for planning by scholars, public authorities, legislatures, cor-

Reprinted with permission from *FUTURES* (August 1989). © 1989 Butterworth & Co. (Publishers) Ltd., UK. This article is based on a presentation made at the 1988 World Futures Studies Federation in Beijing.

porations, one-issue lobbies, and citizens' groups. Simulation techniques are routinely taught in schools of planning and public affairs. Environmental trouble that can be foreseen only in the calculations of nuclear physicists or atmospheric chemists has come to be cover-story fare. People by the millions now use popularized models of the future as guidance on whether to have babies, practice safe sex, buy aerosol hair spray, or even plan a picnic for the day after tomorrow.

Peering into the future is thus accepted, unassailable in its purpose if not in its multiple modes of analysis. "Futurist" is now a mostly respected self-designation; it has even been used as a corporate job description. And all of this has happened in about a quarter of a century.

To call oneself a futurist requires no special credentials, so the tag did attract some strange bedfellows. At a 1980 meeting in Toronto billed modestly as the "First Global Conference on the Future," I was accosted during a coffee break by a dishevelled young man who wanted to know whether I loved Jesus (which I did) and was ready (which I wasn't) for the end of the world the following Tuesday. But at the end of that same meeting, Maurice Strong, the Canadian millionaire and environmental executive, restored my perspective with his closing comment: "The bad news is that the world is coming to an end. The good news is—not yet, and not necessarily."

Sirens to resist

Despite the burgeoning use of fast computers to help answer "what if" questions, "the intellectual construction of a likely future is a work of art," as one of the early pioneers, Bertrand de Jouvenel, wrote in 1967. He called it not planning or forecasting, but "the art of conjecture."

Those who would peer into the future have to learn to turn aside from some tempting siren songs.

One siren lures the futurist to commit the original statistical sin, which is to mistake current megatrends for human destiny. In the early 1970s it was widely believed that we were about to run out of food, soil, energy and fresh water. We haven't yet—partly, to be sure, because the havoc-criers cried havoc.

Another siren tells us that what cannot be counted is an "externality"—that is, a disturbingly relevant factor that does not fit into our current mode of analysis, and so is shelved to think about some other time. But of course the real world is not neatly quantitative. What cannot be counted will often count more than what can.

Yet another siren teaches that "resources" are "natural." Some dedicated number-crunchers still do not consider knowledge, imagination, invention and innovation as resources, perhaps because they are too hard to measure. But in the advanced countries, and increasingly in all countries, information is the primary raw material for economic and social development. It will now play the role in the march of civilization that physical labor, land, bronze, iron, metals and energy once played.

An early illusion, now discredited, was that "the future" was a new subject, a new field of knowledge, a new discipline of inquiry—to be captured in a new kind of academic department. In the flush of the early successes of space exploration, there arose a similar delusion, that outer space was a new subject, to be distinguished from others by developing its own language and its own academic high priests. It did not take long for the space enthusiasts to realize that space was not a new subject but a new place, a fascinating and hostile environment presenting new challenges to all the familiar fields and disciplines such as physics and materials science and engineering and medicine and nutrition and psychology and economics and law. The study of the future, at its best, has likewise developed as a fresh angle of vision on the whole range of human knowledge—and a new reason to thread together the compartmentalized discipline into which we have divided the life of the mind.

The avoidance of all these temptations leads one to avoid trying to predict a unique and inevitable future, and to practice instead what we would now call "imaging"—constructing alternative futures as a basis for working back from a preferred outcome to what we ought to be doing, starting tomorrow morning, to bring it about That is why it makes sense to think about what hasn't happened yet as a plural noun, as in "World Futures Studies Federation," and the name of this journal.

But the prime temptation is always lurking in the wings Amidst the rapid progress in the techniques and technologies of simulation, one constant remains. Among the conceivable future for a person, group, nation or civilization, it is still the dire threats—the nuclear holocaust, the poisoned Earth, the atmospheric heat trap—that win the popularity contest.

The danger of accentuating the negative is that each new scientific discovery, each technological innovation, each new theory of society, impacts on the popular mind as trouble to be avoided, with no corresponding opportunity to be grasped. That mindset could paralyze the collective will to tackle the new kinds of problems that pose the greatest threats to the human species. These are the problems (global warming and AIDS are examples both current and choice) that are not only global in their reach but also behavioral in their solution—that is, they will require literally millions of people to stop doing something familiar, or do something different, or both.

What matters?

In 1988 James Dator, Secretary General of the World Futures Studies Federation, returned from a visit to Australia with news of a poster advertising the prospect that the "greenhouse effect" might cause an irreversible rising of the world's oceans. The poster was large and blue; it depicted the famous "sails" of the Sydney Opera House—the only things visible above the risen water. At the top of the poster, this legend:

If you act as though it matters and it doesn't matter, then it doesn't matter. But if you act as though it doesn't matter and it matters, then it matters.

What is it that matters, to those of us who respect the future? What matters is that the great transformations of our time are still driven primarily by the "inner logic" of scientific discovery and technological innovation. That logic is simple: the more we can discover, the better off we shall be.

Almost a century before Newton, in 1597, Francis Bacon had speculated (also in Latin) that "knowledge is power." Imbedded in the logic of science and technology is the buoyant optimism of Newton's harmonious equations: the orbiting planets of power which knowledge creates will somehow not collide with each other to the detriment of the human species. The logic is linear: as we decipher the riddles of nature, we must naturally give thought to the technologies the new science makes possible; because the new technologies are possible they also must be necessary; if the new technologies enable us to make new machines and processes, we must assuredly design, construct and deploy them.

But nowadays the mood is different. Modern societies no longer stand still for the uncritical translation of scientific insights into social dogmas. Science and technology have produced so much dirt and smog and ugliness, so many explosions and crashes in fail-safe systems, so much wasted weaponry and undisposable waste, that popular resistance to the inner logic of the scientific method grows louder every year.

Evidence of the new, ambivalent mood—still mesmerized by science, but newly wary of technology—is all around us. It has penetrated party politics (the Greens), business (baby formula, car safety, smoking), public policy (clean water, acid rain, smog, aircraft noise), and international relations (arms control and agreements to restrain pollution and promote aircraft safety). Thinkers in developing countries have been talking (though their governments are not doing much) about alternative modes of development that would not require the waste and unfairness which seem, in industrial society, to be the handmaidens of "progress." From time to time, a major man-bites-dog decision is taken *not* to manufacture and deploy something new even though we know how: the US Senate check-mated the project for a supersonic transport (the SST), and the two superpowers agreed not to deploy anti-ballistic missile systems.

What emerges as a prospect, 300 years after Newton, is a creative combination of human limits and human opportunities—the opportunities presenting themselves only if the human species controls itself. The emerging ethic of ecology is an interlocking system of human self-control—not "limits to growth" but limits to thoughtlessness, unfairness and conflict.

Fatal dangers, fateful opportunities

Consider four concurrent science and technology revolutions, each in its uncaring ambivalence carrying fatal dangers and fateful opportunities for the human species.

Nuclear power   A dimensional change in explosive power has created perils without precedent whether on purpose (Hiroshima, Nagasaki) or by mistake (Chernobyl). It has also created alternative sources of energy and additional tools for medicine. Yet, by making it possible to invent weapons too powerful to use, science seems, by an accident of frightfulness, to have clamped a lid on the scale of violence, for the first time in world history.

The nuclear part of military strategy can now be best understood as a complex and expensive "information game" in which the military unusability of nuclear weapons enhances both lesser forms of violence and non-military forms of power.

Biotechnology   A breakthrough in deciphering the inherited information in our genes has provided us with a vast array of biotechnologies. Some of the applications are unimaginably frightful new capacities for genocide. But the same discovery has also pointed to means of multiplying the productivity of plants and animals, ways to make protein cheap and abundant, to produce human insulin from bacteria, to manufacture more targetable antibiotics and vaccines against previously intractable viruses, and even to correct birth defects in an individual fetus.

At a Hong Kong meeting last year on biotechnology's likely impacts on international governance, I listened to world-class experts as they speculated that biotechnology could (if we don't let ourselves be mesmerized by its dark potentials) be good news for "growth with fairness" worldwide. The inherent nature of biological resources, and the fact that most of the world's rich supply of biomass—and most of the world's solar radiation, too—is concentrated in the so-called "poorer" parts of the world, holds promise that a world society focusing sharply on the constructive uses of the bioresource can be a fairer world.

Climate change Atmospheric gases, the products of industrial civilization, may now be the agents of large-scale, unprecedented change in the global climate. This global change could double back on human civilization, radically redistributing moisture and, in the span of a single lifetime, inundate not only Sydney but most of the world's great seaports. For the first time in world history we, *Homo sapiens*, the self-proclaimed wisest of the species, are able to do more to our natural environment than nature does to, and for, us. An ironic anonymous couplet says it all:

Strange that man should make a list of living things in danger. Why he fails to list himself is really even stranger.

But ... the prospect of global environmental damage, the product of past breakthroughs in science and technology, is also generating new breakthroughs in thinking about global cooperation to avoid it. Shared environments such as outer space, the atmosphere, the oceans, and (so far) Antarctica can be neither owned nor divided; they constitute a natural commons. Unlike the classic commons, where excessive use (an overpopulation of sheep on a shared pasture) led to its "enclosure," the tragedy of the global commons would be its competitive mismanagement: so littering it with waste, debris and chemicals that, still undivided and unenclosed, it became unusable for all humankind. The cooperative governance of the global commons is one of the great tasks of international statesmanship in the generation just ahead.

Informatization of society Above all, the convergence of two separate lines of science and technology—faster computers and more reliable telecommunications—is creating societies where the dominant resource is information, the dominant activity no longer the production and exchange of things but the production and sharing of symbols.

Shortly before her death in 1946, Gertrude Stein, reaching for aphorisms even in her decline, complained that "Everybody gets so much information all day long that they lose their common sense." To regain our common sense, the informatization of society requires us to rethink the very fundaments of our philosophy—rethink an economics in which value inheres in scarcity, rethink governance based on secrecy, rethink laws based on ownership, and rethink management based on hierarchy.

The good news is that information, our newly dominant resource, is clearly more accessible than any of the resources that have heretofore been dominant in world history. The spread of education is bound to erode the power that once accrued to the few who were "in the know." That has to be advantageous for the disadvantaged world-wide—if they don't get discouraged by listening to downbeat experts who, mistaking current trends for destiny, note that establishments left over from the industrial age are doing their best to enhance their power with the new information technologies, and assume they will succeed.

What works

Let me make my critique quite explicit. Futures studies risks being preoccupied with what's wrong with the picture. The study of international relations focuses on riots and their suppression, military takeovers, drug traffic, corporate raids, financial psychoses, arms races, wars and rumors of wars. Yet if you stand back and look at the whole scene, you see all kinds of international systems and arrangements that are working more or less the way they are supposed to work:

Weather forecasting: the World Weather Watch daily merges observations from over 100 countries with cloud pictures and wind and moisture data from satellites. You use the results in your personal planning, every day of the year.

Infectious diseases such as smallpox and diphtheria have been wiped out, malaria and others tackled, by combining medical science with an information system that requires the cooperation of almost every nation on Earth. Next on this never-ending agenda: AIDS.

Civil aviation: planes of all nations use each other's air space, control towers, and airfields with astonishingly few mishaps.

Radio waves are divided up among all uses and users by international agreement. What a mess our radio and TV reception, our satellite phone connections, our space programs—and our military preparedness—would be if the frequency spectrum were a free market!

A worldwide agricultural research network has already generated the Green revolution and is working hard, through plant and animal breeding, to follow up with the "gene revolution."

To protect the Earth's ozone shield, 50 nations agreed in September 1988 to slow down the use of such ozone eaters as chlorofluorocarbons.

Antarctica: a dozen nations (later joined by a few others) agreed in 1959 to suspend their national claims and open up an entire continent to scientific research, banning nuclear tests or waste disposal in the huge frozen no-man's-land.

Outer space: nations have agreed by treaty that outer space and its bodies (including the Moon) are "the common heritage of mankind."

Law of the Sea: by an extraordinary act of consensus, the world's
nations spent 15 years rewriting ocean law in a book-length
treaty, leaving only one loose end (the Reagan administration's
last-minute decision to oppose an international regime for the
deep seabed).

Refugees: the United Nations High Commissioner for Refugees
has been doing an energetic and imaginative job as catalyst and
coordinator, stimulating actions that have saved millions of people from international homelessness.

It is hard to know where to stop. This illustrative list leaves out
arms control, which is just beginning to get somewhere; alliances
(NATO is in trouble, but this is the agony of success) and other regional pacts; the World Bank, the Children's Fund and other parts
of the United Nations' unfinished war on poverty; transnational
corporations, which do so many things (not without controversy)
that governments seem unable to do even when they work together;
and global media events like Live Aid, the concert for Bangladesh,
and "We are the World."

   I have also left out something hard to classify: the increasingly
global flow of information. The fusion of computers and telecommunications is unsettling most governments, investors, speculators
and criminals. But it certainly does "work."

Ingredients of success
Why does international cooperation work—when it does?
   At the University of Minnesota's Humphrey Institute, Senior
Fellow Geri Joseph and I have worked with graduate students to
analyze how the programs that work are working, and why. Here is
an interim report on the priceless ingredients of "success."

1. There is a consensus on desired outcomes. People can agree
    that smallpox is a threat to all, more accurate weather fore-
    casts are needed, enclosed seas should be cleaned up, civil air-
    craft should not collide, somebody should help refugees.
    There is no comparable consensus about armaments, trade or
    money.
2. No one loses. There was no INF treaty until each side con-
    cluded that its security could actually be enhanced by getting
    rid of unusable weapons systems.
3. Sovereignty is "pooled." When a nation cannot act effectively
    without combining its resources, imagination and technology
    with those of other nations, such cooperation does not mean
    giving up sovereignty but pooling it—that is, using it to-
    gether to avoid losing it separately.
4. Cooperation is stimulated by "a cocktail of fear and hope."

Fear alone produces irrational, sometimes aggressive behavior. Hope alone produces good-hearted but unrealistic advocacy. Reality-based fear and hope, combined, seem to provide the motivation to cooperate.

5. People, not bureaucratic structures, make things happen. In each case of successful international cooperation, a crucial role has been played by a few key individuals able to lead, inspire, share knowledge and generate a climate of trust that brushes off the distrust still prevailing in other domains.

6. Key roles are played by nongovernments—scientific academies, research institutes, women's groups, international companies, and "experts" who do not feel the need to act as representatives of their governments.

7. Information technologies are of the essence. Needs for complex data processing and rapid, reliable communication seem to be common to the success stories in international cooperation.

8. Flexible, uncentralized systems work best. The more complicated the task and the more diverse the players, the more necessary it is to spread the work around so that many kinds of people are unleashed to be entrepreneurs, "public" as well as "private."

9. Educated "local talent" is essential. Especially where developing countries play a big part, cooperation works best when they use their own talent to do their own thing. The colonial days are past: imported experts should not plan to stay.

10. In all the examples of international cooperation we studied, the USA was a key player. The other side of the coin is equally evident: when the US government is dead in the water—most recently, in the decade of the 1980s—international cooperation slackens and loses momentum.

A future that works

In futures studies, as in other modes of policy analysis, gloomy preoccupation with what might go wrong can paralyze needed action right now. Rosy sentimentality can also induce paralysis, that of Pollyanna: We'll surely manage to get out of the rut we're in, so why bother to push?

What is left is the role of practical visionary, a function paradoxical enough to have appealed to Lao Tzu.

One practical visionary, the Norwegian explorer Thor Heyerdahl, says he has edited his philosophy of life down to seven words: "Translate ideas into events, to serve people." It is the world's highest calling. But the starting point for thought leading to action is the imaging of a future that works—and that's where futures studies come in.

Ten Do's and Don'ts of Forecasting and Planning

Roy Amara

Editor's note: This article is an excerpt from a longer work in which Roy Amara considered the first ten-year forecast of the Institute for the Future (IFTF), generated in 1978. The first portion of the original article summarized the IFTF forecast and discussed the "hits and misses." The ten do's and don'ts presented here are based on Amara's analysis of the IFTF forecast.

From our decade of *Ten-Year Forecasts* and our 20 years of experience with long-range forecasting and planning, it is possible to discern some reasonably clear messages. These are presented not in the form of "external verities" but as 10 useful "rules of thumb."

1. Don't be a vacuum cleaner

Stated differently, the clear message is to avoid collecting every speck of information that comes across your field of view unless you know exactly how you are going to use it. How do you decide what your focus should be? How can you avoid missing something that may later turn out to be critically important? And, given your objectives, where are the greatest uncertainties?

Let me acknowledge at the outset that there are no easy answers to these questions. Only incomplete and piecemeal solutions are available. In their most general form, the questions relate to the selection of agendas. They simply confirm what we already know—it is much easier to do something with a set of items that is given than to assure yourself that you have the right set to begin with.

Excerpted from "What We Have Learned about Forecasting and Planning"; reprinted with permission from *FUTURES* (August 1988). © 1988 Butterworth & Co. (Publishers) Ltd., UK.

More technically, it is the difference between decision making, or the act of choosing from among a set of alternatives, and problem solving, or the generation of the field from which the choice is to be made. We confront such problems in a variety of forms, such as in selecting a set of "key" variables, choosing the "right" experts, or generating a set of options. Agenda selection is related to, but goes somewhat beyond, information filtering or getting the right information to the right person at the right time. It is similarly related to, but different from, the discovery of patterns in raw intelligence or data. Agenda selection is the act of making a first stab at modelling a situation or getting some sense of what is important and of "what is connected to what."

If not a vacuum cleaner, then what should we strive to be? The answer is a set of lenses or filters. The number, shape, and size of the lenses are dictated by the question "What for?" In other words, how will the collected information be used?

A simple example (see Figure 1) illustrates the process. Let's assume that one of your objectives is to make forecasts of market share and sales for a product or service. These variables are influenced by total demand and the number and effectiveness of competitors, and these, in turn, may depend on real GNP growth and on interest rates. Here, a set of three lenses may be visualized—at the corporate, industry, and macro levels. However it is done, some sequence of logic needs to be constructed between those variables of interest to you and those that affect their behavior. This is one way of selecting an initial agenda that may be modified in successive iterations. (The loop will be closed in Guideline 10.)

The important point is that unless you construct the equivalent of a set of lenses or filters, you will soon find yourself hopelessly lost. Not only will you run the danger of information overload, but you also will have little basis for separating the wheat from the chaff. Clearly, a balance needs to be struck between adequacy and complexity. We cannot represent a complex system in its entirety or we will be defeated in our ability to understand it. Instead, we must

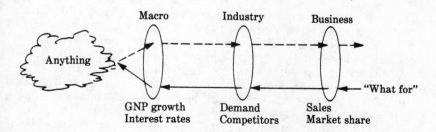

Figure 1. The need for lenses and filters.

necessarily abstract what we consider to be an essential set of variables, recognizing that in doing so we are thereafter working with an incompletely specified system.

2. Don't substitute error for uncertainty

This is how forecasting usually gets its bad name. What is recognized by this simple guideline is that some variables are more uncertain than others. For those key variables with the greatest uncertainty, you should not try—however great the temptation—to be a hero. Otherwise, you are likely to suffer the fate that Andy Warhol predicted for many of us—stardom for 15 minutes.

Where our state of knowledge is such that considerable uncertainty remains about a variable, decision makers would be happier knowing the sports ground in which the game is to be played, rather than the score, which is likely to be wrong. For example, will GNP growth rates be between 2% and 2½% or between 2½% and 3%? Are inflation or interest rates going to be in the range of 0–5%, 5–10%, or in the double-digit range? Is the political climate likely to shift towards the right or left?

3. At times, lean against the wind

Other ways exist for combating the pseudodeterminism that accompanies most forecasting. One of the most effective is to question conventional wisdom—at times. Since conventional wisdom is not always wrong, great care needs to be exercised in picking one's targets. Unfortunately, no general rules exist. But the extent and speed with which we all have access to the same information have increased markedly, with the result that we generally find ourselves rushing to the same corner of the room. Under these circumstances, leaning against the wind can pay off handsomely. Some examples may serve to illustrate how this may be done.

One way is to question so-called inconsistencies—conditions that could not exist simultaneously. In the late 1970s and early 1980s, we were told that high inflation and high unemployment could not exist at the same time (remember the Phillips Curve?).[1] This law was repealed by the OPEC shocks of 1973 and 1979, when both inflation and unemployment soared. The US economy had simply become more open without our appreciating it. Similarly, a low dollar and high trade deficits could not coexist. However, once foreign producers have established a toehold in the US market, they will raise prices and customers will pay premium prices for some time. So, in the long run we may all be dead, but in the short run a falling dollar is not inconsistent with high import levels. How about prosperity and high budget deficits? This inconsistency occurred because Ronald Reagan lost his gamble on tax reduction. He hit the inner boundaries of social spending cuts beyond which Congress—

with the support of the US electorate—would not budge.

Another way of leaning against the wind is to turn an existing trend on its head by creating an "untrend." For example, conventional wisdom indicates that labor shortages in the USA may be likely in the near future because of sharp drops in fertility rates in previous decades. But will these be cushioned, or will they occur at all if the USA experiences unexpected levels of immigration, or a very slow-growing economy, or sharp improvements in white-collar productivity? Another example can be drawn from prevailing US tax policy aimed at reducing tax schedules across the board. How likely is it that a shift may occur towards a "maximizing tax" policy that hits upper- and middle-income households as well as businesses in order to finance some deferred social agendas (for example, education and health)? And, finally, should we question the maxim that Japan excels in manufacturing ("everything is made in Japan") when, in fact, labor costs in some sectors of the USA are below those of Japan and when we see a host of formidable new competitors (for example, the newly industrializing countries) on the manufacturing horizon?

4. Hedge forecasts with possible surprises

Surprises are by definition events or trends that we perceive to be of low probability. We are particularly interested in those surprises that could have a large impact if they were to occur. Identifying such possible surprises is simply another way of compensating for the fact that we are necessarily working with incompletely specified systems. What they do is give decision makers the option of buying commensurate insurance in order to limit (but never completely to avoid) the downside risks of a chosen mainline strategy.

Surprises can stem from the unexpected reversal of current trends. For example, energy prices could begin to climb steeply or an oil price shock similar to those in the 1970s could occur. Although the latter is somewhat less likely, the former falls into the category of "when," not "if." Another example of a trend reversal is the possibility that US defense budgets may not just flatten out but may decline in real terms for a number of years. Real reductions of 5% per year can contribute greatly to easing budget deficits or to shifting expenditures to other higher priority areas.

Surprises may also result from the effects of unspectacular trends that persist for long periods of time. For example, US manufacturing—which has been holding its own through healthy productivity increases—may now also benefit considerably from the dollar's decline. The positive effects would extend far beyond the manufacturing sector *per se*, into those activities that bring goods to market, sell them, and service them—estimated to include well over 60% of the US labor force. Also falling into this category as a possible surprise are the effects that would result from the persistence of trade deficits. Even with a declining dollar, the level of imports into the USA could remain high for a long time simply because the USA no longer manufactures many products—cameras, videocassette recorders, magnetrons for microwave ovens, and so forth.

Finally, surprises can sneak up on us when we are not looking—even though we should have known better. Many demographically driven trends fall into this category, as do trends that derive from cyclic swings in political philosophy or national moods. A particular cycle that may begin in the 1990s is the swing towards a period of greater activism by the US government—resembling in this respect the 1960s. Even this kind of 30-year cyclic swing may be demographically driven, since the periodicity corresponds approximately to the span of a generation.

5. Look for breakpoints and discontinuities

Most forecasters dream about forecasting a major breakthrough in a long-term trend. However, not many taste the experience because it combines the elements of keen insight, high courage and considerable luck. A few examples will illustrate why discontinuities are so difficult to forecast.

The first example that comes to mind is stock market behavior, particularly that of October 19, 1987. This discontinuity was as sharp and unexpected as any can be. What particularly caught our attention, however, was that the stock market had been considered by some as the classic example of random walk or "efficient market," where stock prices continuously discount all new information and all movement is random, with no relationship to what has occurred before. A more relevant problem now is to determine what part of stock price movement is truly random and what part is due to the behavior of some existing—but poorly understood—underlying structure. The best current guess is that the market may represent an outstanding example of so-called "non-linear dynamic systems"—that is, systems that occasionally register very large changes in output (for example, discontinuities) for very small changes in input. Many complex physical systems and most social, economic and political systems exhibit such behavior at times. The favorite current culprits to explain stock market behavior are stock futures (for example, portfolio insurance) and program trading, each operating to create the kind of reinforcing feedback that can send a system into violent swings or unstable oscillations. But no one knows for sure, since we don't know enough about the underlying structure or the key driving forces. To make matters worse, the entire system is a moving target where the ground rules—the structure and drivers—are constantly changing.

The second example illustrating a major recent discontinuity is drawn from the class of physical systems, where the fundamental ground rules are not in a constant state of change. After about 75 years of continuous and gradual change, superconductive transition temperatures in 1986 shot through the ceiling. This discovery not only was unexpected, but it came from an unexpected quarter. Even here, however, large elements of human choice and luck were present. J. Bednorz and K. Muller elected to search for superconductivity among a class of materials that normally conducts electricity very poorly—namely, ceramics. As a result, attention is now sharply focused on a wholesale revamping of our perceptions and theories about the underlying physical structures that govern the physics of superconductivity.

6. Focus on underlying driving forces

A clear message to this point is that, aside from a focus on structure and drivers, no analytical silver bullets are likely to be found in forecasting discontinuities. We need to discover and understand the underlying elements affecting variables of interest. Perhaps this is just another way of adapting a planning aphorism to forecasting: "Forecasting is everything; the forecast is nothing."

Actually, both the forecast and the driving forces are equally important. Without the "logics" of the forecast, others are not likely to buy into a forecast; likewise, even the best picture of underlying dynamics will be sterile unless it provides a test (for example, a forecast) of its efficacy. An effective way to begin identifying driving forces is to focus one's attention on the single most important driver. For corporate restructuring the most important driver may be foreign competition; for diffusion of personal computers in business it may be perceived payback; and for the growth of small business it may be baby-boom growth rates.

7. Look for clusters of drivers

Driving forces do not normally act singly but in clusters. Indeed, one of the most difficult tasks is to limit the set of drivers to a so-called key set. Furthermore, it is precisely the interaction of drivers that provides clues on underlying structure.

Using the example of "growth of small business" (see Figure 2), we illustrate how the rate of growth of baby boomers is disaggregated into demand and supply branches and how these interact with two others—the downsizing of government and corporate restructuring. The resultant growth of small business is thus due to the interplay of several demand components with a dominant supply variable—namely, the growing number of baby boomers willing to try their hand at some form of entrepreneurship.

8. Translate environmental forecasts into business issues

So far, our attention has focused almost exclusively on environmental or core areas—demography, labor force, values and lifestyles, economy, resources, technology, and so forth. The notable exception was in Guideline 1, when the need to act as a logic lens was described and when the "what for" starting point was couched in such terms as market share and sales volume.

Environmental forecasts need to be translated or transformed into forms that have more direct meaning to business functions (see Figure 3). A vehicle that has proved effective is the business issue framed in the form of a threat or opportunity. Conceptually, the process is illustrated by the matrix (or fishnet) in Figure 3. Entering horizontally from the left and exiting vertically down, three examples are shown—the "single cell" issue illustrates how applications of IT to distribution channel systems can be used to achieve competitive marketing advantage; the "diagonal" issue deals with developments in medical technology and the growing demand for convenience combining to open up opportunities for home testing and diagnostic devices; and the vertical, "four-cell" issue illustrates how the diffusion of personal computers, the growing desire for auton-

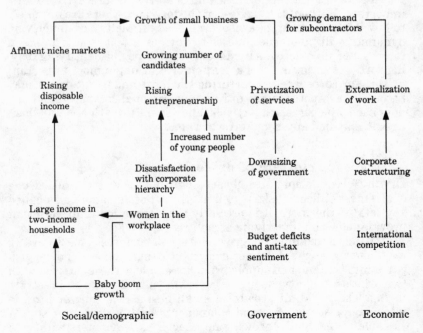

Figure 2. Growth of small businesses.

omy in the workplace, increasing foreign competition, and the slow-ing growth of the labor force can act jointly to spur the demand for new workplace alternatives and structures. Alternatively, if the fishnet analogy is used, each issue represents a way of reaching in to pick up and reconfigure the net.

9. Don't be fooled by the diffusion curve

Figure 4 shows two, now-familiar curves of "percentage of adop-tion" of a technology with the passage of time. One of these—as-sumed to be actual—shows the long period of time over which some technologies diffuse to high levels of adoption and many others that never go on to fulfill their early promise. The other curve—the per-ceived trajectory—is unfortunately the one we carry around in our heads in the early stages of many technologies. This perceived curve differs from the actual in two important respects—it is steadily in-creasing, and it grows in a much shorter period of time. What it ignores is that raw technological capabilities (e.g., robots, speech recognition, videotex), no matter how attractive, do not translate immediately into the adoption for a variety of reasons—unattrac-tive perceived cost/benefit ratios, unanticipated problems, institu-tional inertia, and the need for incremental *in situ* adaptation of a

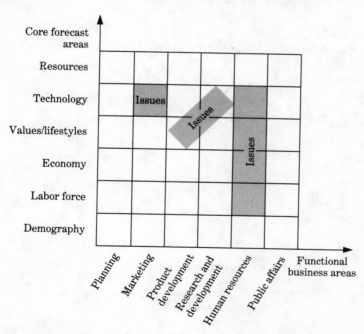

Figure 3. Translating environmental forecasts into issues.

technology. The number of instances in which adoption rates have been overestimated in the short run is legion, including natural language systems, vision systems, videophone, videodiscs, and two-way cable. The result is the usual hype gap in the early stages of a technology shown in Figure 5.

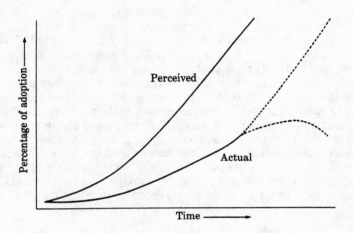

Figure 4. Diffusion curves, perceived and actual.

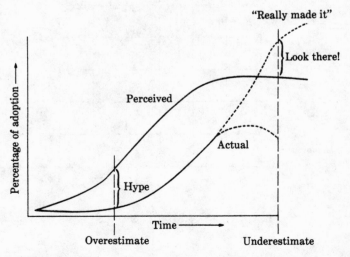

Figure 5. Diffusion curve, underestimates and overestimates.

The opposite effect is the norm at the other end of the diffusion curve for technologies that do make the grade. Often, humbled by the early failures of overestimated adoption rates, we make the opposite kind of error in the latter stages of adoption. As a successful technology slowly works its way through greater acceptance—and may also be transformed in the process (for example, by new applications)—it becomes less visible. At some point, we discover that it has been integrated so successfully into our lives that we have now badly underestimated adoption rates. Recent examples include the diffusion of cable TV, videocassette recorders and microwave ovens. It is somewhat surprising how often we tend to repeat these two types of non-compensating errors.

10. Keep asking "So what?"

In our 10th and final guideline, we will close the loop started in Guideline 1. Figure 6 shows the progression from "What for?" to selection of particular key variables. Armed with the targeted information, the loop is now closed by posing the question "So what?" Does the acquired information serve the purposes it was intended to? What additional information is now required? What is connected to what? How? Now the basically iterative nature of the process becomes clearly visible as "What for?" and "So what?" merge together. Also, the two-sided nature of the process is evident as linkages are built among environmental (or macro), industry and business variables.

The logical lens system of Figure 6 is not quite the appropriate metaphor for this kind of process. A more appropriate and accurate one is the computer. Collapsing the model characterized by the lens system into the computer, the integration of planning and doing makes the two almost indistinguishable. Through computer simulation, a wide variety of business activities can be represented, including complex manufacturing operations as well as more traditional

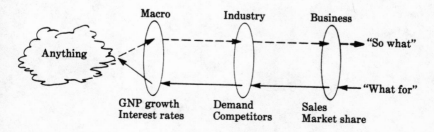

Figure 6. Closing the loop from "What for" to "So what."

functions involving capital investment choices and staff allocation decisions. Results are not only provided virtually instantaneously but also in easy-to-comprehend graphics and animated video.

The other related change created by the closer integration of planning and doing is to make planning itself less visible. Planners will increasingly become part of operational units (i.e., doing). The recent shrinkage of corporate staffs and the move of planners to operating divisions are cases in point. The function of planning does not disappear—it simply returns to its original home. An important by-product of this change is that the organizational and conceptual distance between those with vision (that is, the visionaries) and those who make things happen (that is, the doers) is shortened. As a result, decision-making loops can become tighter, since ideas can be implemented more quickly and feedback on performance can be more quickly assessed.

We can thus have two kinds of integration between planning and doing—conceptual and operational. Conceptually, the cycle between planning and doing becomes more compressed. Operationally, planning and doing become organizationally integrated.

1. A curve whereby unemployment and
    inflation are inversely related—if in-
    flation rises, unemployment falls.

PART 2

Critical
Connections

As the World Turns

— Robert B. Reich

Between 1978 and 1987, the poorest fifth of American families became eight percent poorer, and the richest fifth became 13 percent richer. That leaves the poorest fifth with less than five percent of the nation's income, and the richest fifth with more than 40 percent. This widening gap can't be blamed on the growth in single-parent, lower-income families, which in fact slowed markedly after the late 1970s. Nor is it due mainly to the stingy social policy of the Reagan years. Granted, Food Stamp benefits have dropped in real terms by about 13 percent since 1981, and many states have failed to raise benefits for the poor and unemployed to keep up with inflation. But this doesn't come close to accounting for the growing inequality. Rather, the trend is connected to a profound change in the American economy as it merges with the global economy. And because the merging is far from complete, this trend will not stop of its own accord anytime soon.

It is significant that the growth of inequality shows up most strikingly among Americans who have jobs. Through most of the postwar era, the wages of Americans at different income levels rose at about the same pace. Although different workers occupied different steps on the escalator, everyone moved up together. In those days poverty was the condition of *jobless* Americans, and the major economic challenge was to create enough jobs for everyone. Once people were safely on the work force escalator, their problems were assumed to be over. Thus "full employment" became a liberal rallying cry, while conservatives fretted over the inflationary tendencies of a full-employment economy.

In recent years working Americans have been traveling on two escalators—one going up, the other going down. In 1987 the average hourly earnings of nonsupervisory workers, adjusted for inflation, were lower than in any year since 1966. Middle-level managers fared much better, although their median real earnings were only slightly above the levels of the 1970s. Executives, however, did spectacularly well. In 1988 alone, CEOs of the hundred largest publicly held industrial corporations received raises averaging almost 12 percent. The remunerations of lesser executives rose almost as much, and executives of smaller companies followed close behind.

Between 1978 and 1987, as the real earnings of unskilled workers were declining, the real incomes of workers in the securities industry (investment bankers, arbitrageurs, and brokers) rose 21 percent. Few investment bankers pocket anything near the $50 million lavished yearly upon the partners of Kohlberg, Kravis, Roberts & Company, or the $550 million commandeered in 1988 by Michael Milken, but it is not unusual for a run-of-the-mill investment banker to bring home comfortably over a million dollars. Partners in America's largest corporate law firms are comparatively deprived, enjoying average yearly earnings of only $400,000 to $1.2 million.

Meanwhile, the number of impoverished *working* Americans climbed by nearly two million, or 23 percent, between 1978 and 1987. The number who worked full time and year round but were poor climbed faster, by 43 percent. Nearly 60 percent of the 20 million people who now fall below the Census Bureau's poverty line are from families with at least one member in full-time or part-time work.

The American economy, in short, is creating a wider range of earnings than at any other time in the postwar era. The most basic reason, put simply, is that America itself is ceasing to exist as a system of production and exchange separate from the rest of the world. One can no more meaningfully speak of an "American economy" than of a "Delaware economy." We are becoming but a region—albeit still a relatively wealthy region—of a global economy, whose technologies, savings, and investments move effortlessly across borders, making it harder for individual nations to control their economic destinies.

By now Washington officials well understand that the nation's fiscal and monetary policies cannot be set without taking account of the savings that will slosh in or slosh out of the nation in consequence. Less understood is the speed and ease with which new technologies now spread across the globe, from computers in, say, San Jose, to satellite, and then back down to computers in Taiwan. (America's efforts to stop the Japanese from copying our commercial designs and the Soviets from copying our military designs are about equally doomed.) And we have yet to come to terms with the rise of the global corporation, whose managers, shareholders, and employees span the world. Our debates over the future of American jobs still focus on topics like the competitiveness of the American automobile industry or the future of American manufacturing. But these categories are increasingly irrelevant. They assume the existence of a separate American economy in which all the jobs associated with a particular industry, or even more generally with a particular sector, are bound together, facing a common fate.

New technologies of worldwide communication and transportation have redrawn the playing field. American industries no longer compete against Japanese or European industries. Rather, a company with headquarters in the United States, production facilities in Taiwan, and a marketing force spread across many nations competes with another, similarly ecumenical company. So when General Motors, say, is doing well, that probably is good news for a lot of executives in Detroit, and for GM shareholders across the globe, but it isn't necessarily good news for a lot of assembly-line workers in Detroit, because there may, in fact, be very few GM assembly-line workers in Detroit, or anywhere else in America. The welfare of assembly-line workers in Detroit may depend, instead, on the health of corporations based in Japan or Canada.

More to the point: even if those Canadian and Japanese corporations are doing well, these workers may be in trouble. For they are increasingly part of an international labor market, encompassing Asia, Africa, Western Europe—and perhaps, before long, Eastern Europe. Corporations can with relative ease relocate their production centers, and alter their international lines of communication and transportation accordingly, to take advantage of low wages. So American workers find themselves settling for low wages in order to hold on to their jobs. More and more, your "competitiveness" as a worker depends not on the fortunes of any American corporation, or of any American industry, but on what function you serve within the global economy. GM executives are becoming more "competitive" even as GM production workers become less so, because the functions that GM executives perform are more highly valued in the world market than the functions that GM production workers perform.

In order to see in greater detail what is happening to American jobs, it helps to view the work Americans do in terms of functional categories that reflect the real competitive positions of workers in the global economy. Essentially, three broad categories are emerging. Call them symbolic-analytic services, routine production services, and routine personal services.

Symbolic-analytic services are based on the manipulation of information: data, words, and oral and visual symbols. Symbolic analysis comprises some (but by no means all) of the work undertaken by people who call themselves lawyers, investment bankers, commercial bankers, management consultants, research scientists, academics, public-relations executives, real estate developers, and even a few creative accountants. Also: advertising and marketing specialists, art directors, design engineers, architects, writers and editors, musicians, and television and film producers. Some of the manipulations performed by symbolic analysts reveal ways of more efficiently deploying resources or shifting financial assets, or of otherwise saving time and energy. Other manipulations grab money from people who are too slow or naive to protect themselves by manipulation in response. Still others serve to entertain the recipients.

Most symbolic analysts work alone or in small teams. If they work with others, they often have partners rather than bosses or supervisors, and their yearly income is variable, depending on how much value they add to the business. Their work environments tend to be quiet and tastefully decorated, often within tall steel-and-glass buildings. They rarely come in direct contact with the ultimate beneficiaries of their work. When they are not analyzing, designing, or strategizing, they are in meetings or on the telephone—giving advice or making deals. Many of them spend inordinate time in jet planes and hotels. They are articulate and well groomed. The vast majority are white males.

Symbolic analysis now accounts for more than 40 percent of America's gross national product, and almost 20 percent of our jobs. Within what we still term our "manufacturing sector," symbolic-analytic jobs have been increasing at a rate almost three times that of total manufacturing employment in the United States, as routine manufacturing jobs have drifted overseas or been mastered by machines.

The services performed by America's symbolic analysts are in high demand around the world, regardless of whether the symbolic analysts provide them in person or transmit them via satellite and fiber-optic cable. The Japanese are buying up the insights and inventions of America's scientists and engineers (who are only too happy to sell them at a fat profit). The Europeans, meanwhile, are hiring our management consultants, business strategists, and investment bankers. Developing nations are hiring our civil and design engineers; and almost everyone is buying the output of our pop musicians, television stars, and film producers.

It is the same with the global corporation. The central offices of these sprawling entities, headquartered in America, are filled with symbolic analysts who manipulate information and then export their insights via the corporation's far-flung enterprise. IBM doesn't export machines from the United States; it makes machines all over the globe, and services them on the spot. IBM world headquarters, in Armonk, New York, just exports strategic planning and related management services.

Thus has the standard of living of America's symbolic analysts risen. They increasingly find themselves part of a global labor market, not a national one. And because the United States has a highly developed economy, and an excellent university system, they find that the services they have to offer are quite scarce in the context of the whole world. So elementary laws of supply and demand ensure that their salaries are quite high.

These salaries are likely to go even higher in the years ahead, as the world market for symbolic analysis continues to grow. Foreigners are trying to learn these skills and techniques, to be sure, but they still have a long way to go. No other country does a better job of preparing its most fortunate citizens for symbolic analysis than does the United States. None has surpassed America in providing experience and training, often with entire regions specializing in one or another kind of symbolic analysis (New York and Chicago for finance, Los Angeles for music and film, the San Francisco Bay area and greater Boston for science and engineering). In this we can take pride. But for the second major category of American workers—the providers of routine production services—the laws of supply and demand don't bode well.

Routine production services involve tasks that are repeated over and over, as one step in a sequence of steps for producing a finished product. Although we tend to associate these jobs with manufacturing, they are becoming common in the storage and retrieval of information. Banking, insurance, wholesaling, retailing, health care— all employ hordes of people who spend their days processing data, often putting information into computers or taking it out.

Most providers of routine production services work with many other people who do similar work within large, centralized facilities. They are overseen by supervisors, who in turn are monitored by more senior supervisors. They are usually paid an hourly wage. Their jobs are monotonous. Most of these people do not have a college education; they need only be able to take directions and, occasionally, undertake simple computations. Those who deal with metal are mostly white males; those who deal with fabrics or information tend to be female and/or minorities.

Decades ago, jobs like these were relatively well paid. Henry Ford gave his early production workers five dollars a day, a remarkable sum for the time, in the (correct) belief that they and their neighbors would be among the major buyers of Fords. But in recent years America's providers of routine production services have found themselves in direct competition with millions of foreign workers, most of whom are eager to work for a fraction of the pay of American workers. Through the miracle of satellite transmission, even routine data-processing can now be undertaken in relatively poor nations, thousands of miles away from the skyscrapers where the data are finally used. This fact has given management-level symbolic analysts ever greater bargaining leverage. If routine producers living in America don't agree to reduce their wages, then the work will go abroad.

And it has. In 1950 routine production services constituted about 30 percent of our national product and well over half of American jobs. Today such services represent about 20 percent of national product and one-fourth of jobs. And the scattering of foreign-owned factories placed here to circumvent American protectionism isn't going to reverse the trend. So the standard of living of America's routine production workers will likely keep declining. The dynamics behind the wage concessions, plant closings, and union-busting that have become commonplace are not likely to change.

Routine personal services also entail simple, repetitive work, but, unlike routine production services, they are provided in person. Their immediate objects are specific customers rather than streams of metal, fabric, or data. Included in this employment category are restaurant and hotel workers, barbers and beauticians, retail sales personnel, cabdrivers, household cleaners, daycare workers, hospital attendants and orderlies, truck drivers, and—among the fastest-growing of all—custodians and security guards.

Like production workers, providers of personal services are usually paid by the hour, are carefully supervised, and rarely have more than a high school education. But unlike people in the other two categories of work, these people are in direct contact with the ultimate beneficiaries of what they do. And the companies they work for are often small. In fact, some routine personal-service workers turn entrepreneurial. (Most new businesses and new jobs in America come from this sector—now constituting about 20 percent of GNP and 30 percent of jobs.) Women and minorities make up the bulk of routine personal-service workers.

Apart from the small number who strike out on their own, these workers are paid poorly. They are sheltered from the direct effects of global competition, but not the indirect effects. They often compete with illegal aliens willing to work for low wages, or with former or would-be production workers who can't find well-paying production jobs, or with labor-saving machinery (automated tellers, self-service gas pumps, computerized cashiers) dreamed up by symbolic analysts in America and manufactured in Asia. And because they tend to be unskilled and dispersed among small businesses, personal-service workers rarely have a union or a powerful lobby group to stand up for their interests. When the economy turns sour, they are among the first to feel the effects. These workers will continue to have jobs in the years ahead and may experience some small increase in real wages. They will have demographics on their side, as the American work force shrinks. But for all the foregoing reasons, the gap between their earnings and those of the symbolic analysts will continue to grow.

These three functional categories—symbolic analysis, routine production, and routine personal service—cover at least three out of four American jobs. The rest of the nation's work force consists mainly of government employees (including public school teachers), employees in regulated industries (like utility workers), and government-financed workers (engineers working on defense weapons systems), many of whom are sheltered from global competition. One further clarification: some traditional job categories overlap with several functional categories. People called "secretaries," for example, include those who actually spend their time doing symbolic-analytic work closely allied to what their bosses do; those who do routine data entry or retrieval of a sort that will eventually be automated or done overseas; and those who provide routine personal services.

The important point is that workers in these three functional categories are coming to have a different competitive position in the world economy. Symbolic analysts hold a commanding position in an increasingly global labor market. Routine production workers hold a relatively weak position in an increasingly global labor market. Personal-service workers still find themselves in a national labor market, but for various reasons they suffer the indirect effects of competition from workers abroad.

How should we respond to these trends? One response is to accept them as inevitable consequences of change, but try to offset their polarizing effects through a truly progressive income tax, coupled with more generous income assistance—including health insurance—for poor working Americans. (For a start, we might reverse the extraordinarily regressive Social Security amendments of 1983, through which poor working Americans are now financing the federal budget deficit, often paying more in payroll taxes than in income taxes.)

A more ambitious response would be to guard against class rigidities by ensuring that any talented American kid can become a symbolic analyst—regardless of family income or race. Here we see the upside of a globalized economy. Unlike America's old vertically integrated economy, whose white-collar jobs were necessarily limited in proportion to the number of blue-collar jobs beneath them, the global economy imposes no particular limit upon the number of Americans who can sell symbolic-analytic services. In principle, all of America's routine production workers could become symbolic analysts and let their old jobs drift overseas. In practice, of course, we can't even inch toward such a state anytime soon. Not even America's gifted but poor children can aspire to such jobs until the government spends substantially more than it does now to ensure excellent public schools in every city and region to which talented children can go, and ample financial help when they are ready to attend college.

Of course, it isn't clear that even under those circumstances there would be radical growth in the number of Americans who became research scientists, design engineers, musicians, management consultants, or (even if the world needed them) investment bankers and lawyers. So other responses are also needed. Perhaps the most ambitious would be to increase the numbers of Americans who could apply symbolic analysis to production and to personal services.

There is ample evidence, for example, that access to computerized information can enrich production jobs by enabling workers to alter the flow of materials and components in ways that generate new efficiencies. (Shoshana Zuboff's recent book *In the Age of the Smart Machine* carefully documents these possibilities.) Production workers who thus have broader responsibilities and more control over how production is organized cease to be "routine" workers—becoming, in effect, symbolic analysts at a level very close to the production process. The same transformation can occur in personal-service jobs. Consider, for example, the checkout clerk whose computer enables her to control inventory and decide when to reorder items from the factory.

The number of such technologically empowered jobs, of course, is limited by the ability of workers to learn on the job. That means a far greater number of Americans will need good health care (including prenatal and postnatal) and also a good grounding in mathematics, basic science, and reading and communicating. So once again, comfortably integrating the American work force into the new world economy turns out to rest heavily on education.

Education and health care for poor children are apt to be costly. Since poorer working Americans, already under a heavy tax load, can't afford it, the cost would have to be borne by wealthier Americans—who also would have to bear the cost of any income redistribution plans designed to neutralize the polarizing domestic effects of a globalized economy. Thus a central question is the willingness of the more fortunate American citizens—especially symbolic analysts, who constitute the most fortunate fifth, with 40 percent of the nation's income—to bear the burden. But here lies a Catch-22. For as our economic fates diverge, the top fifth may be losing the sense of connectedness with the bottom fifth, or even the bottom half, that would elicit such generosity.

The conservative tide that has swept the land during the last decade surely has many causes, but these economic fundamentals should not be discounted. It is now possible for the most fortunate fifth to sell their expertise directly in the global market, and thus maintain and enhance their standard of living and that of their children, even as that of other Americans declines. There is less and less basis for a strong sense of interclass interdependence. Meanwhile the fortunate fifth have also been able to insulate themselves from the less fortunate, by living in suburban enclaves far removed from the effects of poverty. Neither patriotism nor altruism may be sufficient to overcome these realities. Yet without the active support of the fortunate fifth, it will be difficult to muster the political will necessary for change.

George Bush speaks eloquently of "a thousand points of light" and of the importance of generosity. But so far his administration has set a poor example. A minuscule sum has been budgeted for education, training, and health care for the poor. The president says we can't afford any more. Meanwhile, he pushes a reduction in the capital gains tax rate—another boon to the fortunate fifth.

On withdrawing from the presidential race of 1988, Paul Simon of Illinois said, "Americans instinctively know that we are one nation, one family, and when anyone in that family hurts, all of us hurt." Sadly that is coming to be less and less the case.

The Futures That Have Already Happened

—————————————— Peter Drucker

In five important areas the 1990s will bring far-reaching changes in the social and economic environment, and in the strategies, structure and management of business.

For a start, the world economy will be quite different from what businessmen, politicians and economists still take for granted. The trend towards reciprocity as a central principle of international economic integration has by now become well-nigh irreversible, whether one likes it or not (and I don't).

Economic relations will increasingly be between trading blocks rather than between countries. Indeed, an East Asian bloc loosely organized around Japan and paralleling the EC and North America may emerge during the decade. Relationships will therefore increasingly be conducted through bilateral and trilateral deals in respect both of investment and of trade.

Reciprocity can easily degenerate into protectionism of the worst kind (that's why I dislike it). But it could be fashioned into a powerful tool to expand trade and investment, if—but only if—governments and businessmen act with imagination and courage. In any event, it was probably inevitable. It is the response to the first emergence as a major economic power of a non-western society, Japan.

In the past, whenever a new major economic power appeared, new forms of economic integration soon followed (e.g., the multinational company, which was invented in the middle of the nineteenth century—in defiance of everything Adam Smith and David Ricardo had taught—when the United States and Germany first emerged as major economic powers. By 1913, multinationals had come to control as much of the world's industrial output, maybe more, as they do now). Reciprocity is the way, for better or worse, to integrate a modern but proudly non-western country such as Japan (and the smaller Asian "tigers" that are now following it) into a West-dominated world economy.

The West will no longer tolerate Japan's adversarial trading methods of recent decades—a wall around the home market to protect social structures and traditions, plus a determined push beyond it for world dominance for selected Japanese industries. Yet the western pattern of an autonomous, value-free economy in which economic rationality is the ultimate criterion, is alien to a Confucian society; is indeed seen by it as cultural imperialism. Reciprocity may make possible close economic relationships between culturally distinct societies.

Into alliance

Second, businesses will integrate themselves into the world economy through alliances: minority participations, joint ventures, research and marketing consortia, partnerships in subsidiaries or in special projects, cross-licensing and so on. The partners will be not only other businesses but also a host of non-businesses such as universities, health-care institutions, local governments. The traditional forms of economic integration—trade and the multinational company—will continue to grow, in all likelihood. But the dynamics are shifting rapidly to partnerships based neither on the commodity nexus of trade nor on the power nexus of ownership by multinationals.

There are several reasons for this rapidly accelerating trend:

Many middle-sized and even small businesses will have to become active in the world economy. To maintain leadership in one developed market, a company increasingly has to have a strong presence in all such markets worldwide. But middle-sized and small companies rarely have the financial or managerial resources to build subsidiaries abroad or to acquire them.

Financially, only the Japanese can still afford to go multinational. Their capital costs them around 5% or so. In contrast, European or American companies now pay up to 20% for money. Not many investments, whether in organic growth or in acquisitions, are likely to yield that high a return (except acquisitions by management experts such as Lord Hanson or Warren Buffet, who know how to find a healthy but under-managed business and turn it around). This is especially true of multinational investment, whose risks are increased by currency variations and unfamiliarity with the foreign environment. Financially, it is hard to justify most of the recent acquisitions in America made by European companies. To say that they are "cheap" because of the low dollar is nonsense:

the companies acquired, after all, earn in these low dollars. Only a very big and cash-rich company can really still afford today to go the multinational route.

The major driving forces, however, behind the trend towards alliances are technology and markets. In the past, technologies overlapped little. Electronics people did not need to know much about electrical engineering or about materials. Paper-makers needed to know mainly about paper mechanics and paper chemistry. Telecommunications was self-contained. So was investment banking. Today there is hardly any field in which this is still the case. Not even a big company can any longer get from its own research laboratories all, or even most, of the technology it needs. Conversely, a good lab now produces results in many more areas than can interest even a big and diversified company. So pharmaceutical companies have to ally themselves with geneticists; commercial bankers with underwriters; hardware-makers like IBM with software boutiques. The need for such alliances is the greater the faster a technology grows.

Markets, similarly, are rapidly changing, merging, criss-crossing and overlapping each other. They too are no longer separate and distinct.

Alliances, while needed, are anything but easy. They require extreme—and totally unaccustomed—clarity in respect of objectives, strategies, policies, relationships and people. They also require advance agreement on when and how the alliance is to be brought to an end. For alliances become the more problematic the more successful they are. The best text on them is not to be found in a management book; it is in Winston Churchill's biography of his ancestor the first duke of Marlborough.

Reshaping companies

Third, businesses will undergo more—and more radical—restructuring in the 1990s than at any time since the modern corporate organization first evolved in the 1920s. In 1984, it was treated as sensational news when I pointed out that the information-based organization needs far fewer levels of management than the traditional command-and-control model. By now a great many—maybe most—large American companies have cut management levels by one-third or more. But the restructuring of corporations—middle-sized ones as well as large ones, and, eventually, even smaller ones—has barely begun.

Businesses tomorrow will follow two new rules. One: to move work to where the people are, rather than people to where the work is. Two: to farm out activities that do not offer opportunities for advancement into fairly senior management and professional positions (e.g., clerical work, maintenance, the "back office" in the brokerage house, the drafting room in the large architectural firm, the medical lab in the hospital) to an outside contractor. The corporation, in stockmarket jargon, will be unbundled.

One reason is that this century has acquired the ability to move ideas and information fast and cheaply. At the same time, the great nineteenth-century achievement—the ability to move people—has outlived its usefulness; witness the horrors of daily commuting in most big cities and the smog that hovers over the increasingly clogged traffic arteries. Moving work out to where the people are is already in full train. Few large American banks or insurance companies still process their paperwork in the downtown office. It has been moved out to a satellite in the suburbs (or farther afield—one insurance company ships its claims by air to Ireland every night). Few airlines still locate their reservations computer at the main office or even at the airport.

It may take another "energy crunch" for this trend to become a shock wave. But most work that requires neither decision-making nor face-to-face customer contact (and that means all clerical work) will have been moved out by the end of the decade, at least in western countries; Tokyo and Osaka will take a little longer, I suspect.

(What, by the way, does this mean for the large cities, the children of the nineteenth century's transport revolution? Most of them—London, Paris, New York, Tokyo, Frankfurt—successfully made in this century the transition from manufacturing center to office center. Can they make the next transition—and what will it be? And is the worldwide urban real-estate boom that began in eighteenth-century London at last nearing its end?)

The trend towards "farming out" is also well under way, even in Japan. Most large Japanese hospitals are today cleaned by the local affiliate of the same maintenance contractor that services most American hospitals. Underlying this trend is the growing need for productivity in service work done largely by people without much education or skill. This almost requires that the work be lodged in a separate, outside organization with its own career ladders. Otherwise, it will be given neither enough attention nor importance to ensure the hard work that is needed not just on quality and training, but on work-study, work-flow and tools.

Finally, corporate size will by the end of the coming decade have become a strategic decision. Neither "big is better" nor "small is beautiful" makes much sense. Neither elephant nor mouse nor butterfly is, in itself, "better" or "more beautiful." Size follows function, as a great Scots biologist, D'Arcy Wentworth Thompson, showed in his 1917 classic "On Growth and Form."

A transnational automobile company such as Ford has to be very large. But the automobile industry also has room for a small niche player like Rolls-Royce. Marks & Spencer, for decades the world's most successful retailer, was run as a fair-sized rather than as a large business. So is Tokyo-based Ito-Yokado, arguably the most successful retailer of the past decade. Successful high-engineering companies are, as a rule, middle-sized. But in other industries the middle size does not work well: successful pharmaceutical companies, for instance, tend to be either quite large or quite small. Whatever advantages bigness by itself used to confer on a business have largely been cancelled by the universal availability of management and information. Whatever advantages smallness by itself conferred have largely been offset by the need to think, if not to act, globally. Management will increasingly have to decide on the right size for a business, the size that fits its technology, its strategy and its markets. This is both a difficult and a risky decision—and the right answer is rarely the size that best fits a management's ego.

The challenge to management

Fourth, the governance of companies themselves is in question. The greatest mistake a trend-spotter can make—and one, alas, almost impossible to prevent or correct—is to be prematurely right. A prime example is my 1976 book *The Unseen Revolution*. In it I argued that the shift of ownership in the large, publicly held corporation to representatives of the employee class—i.e., pension funds and unit trusts—constitutes a fundamental change in the locus and character of ownership. It is therefore bound to have profound impact, especially on the governance of companies: above all, to challenge the doctrine, developed since the second world war, of the self-perpetuating professional management in the big company; and to raise new questions regarding the accountability and indeed legitimacy of big-company management.

The Unseen Revolution may be the best book I ever wrote. But it was prematurely right, so no one paid attention to it. Five years later the hostile takeovers began. They work primarily because pension funds are "investors" and not "owners" in their legal obligations, their interests and their mentality. And the hostile takeovers do indeed challenge management's function, its role and its very legitimacy.

The raiders are surely right to assert that a company must be run for performance rather than for the benefit of its management. They are, however, surely wrong in defining "performance" as nothing but immediate, short-term gains for shareholders. This subordinates all other constituencies—above all, managerial and professional employees—to the immediate gratification of people whose only interest in the business is short-term payoffs.

No society will tolerate this for very long. And indeed in the United States a correction is beginning to be worked out by the courts, which increasingly give such employees a "property right" in their jobs. At the same time the large American pension funds (especially the largest, the funds of government employees) are beginning to think through their obligation to a business as a going concern; that is, their obligation as owners.

But the raiders are wrong also because immediate stockholder gains do not, as has now been amply proven, optimize the creation of wealth. That requires a balance between the short term and the long term, which is precisely what management is supposed to provide, and should get paid for. And we know how to establish and maintain this balance.[1]

The governance of business has so far become an issue mainly in the English-speaking countries. But it will soon become an issue also in Japan and West Germany. So far in those two countries the needed balance between the short term and the long has been enforced by the large banks' control of other companies. But in both countries big companies are slipping the banks' leash. And in Japan pension funds will soon own as high a proportion of the nation's large companies as American ones do in the United States; and they are just as interested in short-term stockmarket profits. The governance of business, in other words, is likely to become an issue throughout the developed world.

Again, we may be further advanced towards an answer than most of us realize. In a noteworthy recent article in the *Harvard Business Review*, Professor Michael C. Jansen, of the Harvard Business School, has pointed out that large businesses, especially in the United States, are rapidly "going private." They are putting themselves under the control of a small number of large holders; and in such a way that their holders' self-interest lies in building long-term value rather than in reaping immediate stock-market gains. Indeed, only in Japan, with its sky-high price/earnings ratios, is a public issue of equity still the best way for a large company to finance itself.

Unbundling too should go a long way towards building flexibility into a company's cost structure, and should thus enable it to maintain both short-term earnings and investments in the future. Again the Japanese show the way. The large Japanese manufacturing companies maintain short-term earnings (and employment security for their workers) and long-term investments in the future, by "out-sourcing." They buy from outside contractors a far larger proportion of their parts than western manufacturers usually do. Thus they are able to cut their costs fast and sharply, when they need to, by shifting the burden of short-term fluctuations to the outside supplier.

The basic decisions about the function, accountability and legitimacy of management, whether they are to be made by business, by the market, by lawyers and courts, or by legislators—and, all four will enter the lists—are still ahead of us. They are needed not

because corporate capitalism has failed but because it has succeeded. But that makes them all the more controversial.

The primacy of politics

Fifth, rapid changes in international politics and policies, rather
than domestic economics, are likely to dominate the 1990s. The lode-
star by which the free world has navigated since the late 1940s, the
containment of Russia and of communism, is becoming obsolescent,
because of that policy's very success. And the other basic policy of
these decades, restoration of a worldwide, market-based economy,
has also been singularly successful. But we have no policies yet for
the problems these successes have spawned: the all-but-irreversible
breakup of the Soviet empire, and the decline of China to the point
where it will feature in world affairs mainly because of its weakness
and fragility.

Besides, new challenges have arisen that are quite different:
the environment; terrorism; third-world integration into the world
economy; control or elimination of nuclear, chemical and biological
weapons; and control of the worldwide pollution of the arms race
altogether. They all require concerted, common, transnational action, for which there are few precedents (suppressing the slave
trade, outlawing piracy, the Red Cross are the successful ones that
come to mind).

The past 40 years, despite tensions and crises, were years of
political continuity. The next ten will be years of political discontinuity. Save for such aberrations as the Vietnam era in the United
States, political life since 1945 has been dominated by domestic economic concerns such as unemployment, inflation or nationaliza-
tion/privatization. These issues will not go away. But increasingly
international and transnational political issues will upstage them.

So?

The trends that I have described are not forecasts (for which I have
little use and scant respect); they are, if you will, conclusions. Everything discussed here has already happened; it is only the full
impacts that are still to come. I expect most readers to nod and to
say, "Of course." But few, I suspect, have yet asked themselves:
"What do these futures mean for my own work and my own organization?"

1. The easiest way is for a company to
   have two operating budgets: one,
   short-term, for ongoing operations;
   a second, extending over 3–5 years,
   that covers the work (rarely more
   than 10% or 12% of total expenses)
   needed to build and maintain the company's wealth-producing capacity—
   processes, products, service, markets,
   people. This second, "futures" budget
   should neither be increased in good
   years nor cut in poor ones. This is
   what Japanese companies have been
   doing ever since I first told them about
   it 30 years ago.

Future Information Cities: Japan's Vision

The concept of information cities is not new. It attracted considerable interest from the mid-1960s to the late 1970s, when the "wired city" was envisioned as a central feature of emerging, post-industrial societies.[1]

A number of early pilot systems were mounted, notably HI-OVIS in Japan, Reston in the USA and Milton Keynes in the UK. These were based on state-of-the-art cable television technology, using coaxial cable with capacity for up to 40 video channels, and with a return transmission capability ranging from low-speed data to full video. HI-OVIS was later required with multi-mode optical fiber to provide for two-way video between a selected number of terminals in the system. The applications piloted included on-line polling of current issues, interaction by voice response to televised meetings, distance education, home shopping and working from home.[2]

Against the criteria of user acceptability and cost-effectiveness, none of these pilot systems could be deemed successful, although much was learned about the associated technological and sociological problems. Subsequent trials in France (Biarritz),[3] West Germany[4] and elsewhere were somewhat more effective in that they focused on more limited and specific applications, but again they fell short of expectations.

The 1980s have seen unprecedented advances in telecommunications technology, centered around digital operations, integrated microcircuitry and optical fiber transmission systems. Virtually unlimited transmission capacity is becoming available at ever

Reprinted with permission from *FUTURES* (June 1989). © 1989 Butterworth & Co. (Publishers) Ltd., UK.

diminishing unit cost; the same applies to the storage, retrieval and processing of information. These developments, and the mounting recognition of information technology's key role in supporting economic growth, have revived some of the earlier visions of information-based societies and information cities. It remains to be seen whether a more enlightened understanding of the social issues emerges. This trend is evident in Japan, which has become a world leader in the development and manufacture of information technology (IT). Japan's economic policy is based to a large extent on the future dominance of its information industries, which are forecast to reach 140 trillion yen and account for 20.7% of the nation's GNP by the year 2000.

Communications technology finds particular expression in Japanese urban planning. There is an almost obsessive attachment to the concept of information cities, which feature in the national plans of central government agencies and in the strategic plans of municipalities.

In 1983 the powerful Ministry of International Trade and Industry (MITI) announced its plans for "advanced information cities and new media communities." Eight cities and districts were selected in 1984 for the development of model information systems to serve specified needs. Takasakasaki City, for example, was chosen for the development of a wholesale business center; Yokohama City was targeted for metropolitan redevelopment; Hasse district was selected for industrial development, as an area of major power generation; and Oita City was the chosen site for the creation of a "technopolis."

In the subsequent years to 1987, the number of nominated locations increased to 55. Through its New Media Development Association, MITI assists by providing funding and expertise for these projects through the phases of survey and study, system design, public relations, education and training, R&D (hardware and software), and documentation and coordination. Implementation is the responsibility of the local municipal or prefectural government which handles detailed design and funding, including joint ventures with private sector organizations.

Two other Japanese ministries also support major information projects. In 1983 the Ministry of Posts and Telecommunications (MPT) launched a program for the construction of "teletopias." These were nominated cluster locations serviced by advanced telecommunications facilities—including, in some locations, teleports—giving direct national and international access. To date, 128 teletopias have been nominated. In 1984 the Ministry of Construction inaugurated a study of "city development in line with the information age." Following its report in 1985, a program of "intelligent cities" was announced in 1986 to be funded in part by low-interest loans from the Japan Development Bank and other financial institutions. Municipal governments were invited to apply for intelligent city status and of 40 applications, 22 were selected in 1987, including some rural centers. In 1988, basic plans for seven of these cities were approved, and the process was extended with 14 further provisional designations.

There seems to be little direct coordination between the three ministries; rather they appear to be in competition. The municipalities try to secure the best of all possible worlds, playing one ministry off against another, and providing whatever degree of coordination between ministries is necessary for the solution mix finally adopted.

The overwhelming conviction that IT promises solutions not only to the physical and spatial problems of future urban development, but also to problems of human values and community life, is remarkable in the light of the negative results of Japan's earlier wired-city trials. This apparent contradiction is perhaps symptomatic of a deep-seated ambivalence in the contemporary Japanese psyche, which has arisen as a result of Japan's rapid transition from an ancient to an advanced technological culture and, even more rapidly, from a post-war, devastated and defeated nation to an economic superpower. Pervasive evidence of ambivalence toward Western culture abounds in advertising, fast food, architecture and fashion, to quote just a few of the more obvious examples.

National problems

Despite its unparalleled economic success, Japan today faces some formidable problems. Paradoxically, many of these are the result of that very success.

Balance of payments In 1960 Japan accounted for 3% of world production, while the USA accounted for 32%. By 1985 the USA's contribution had declined to 24% while Japan's had increased to 12%. Today Japan's excess of exports over imports has caused appreciation of the yen to the extent that Japanese goods are too expensive for many of the world's consumers. Not only does Japanese industry urgently need more offshore production, but it also needs new products and new markets, both domestic and overseas.

Basic research While Japan is unsurpassed in applied R&D, it is remarkably limited in basic research. Few of the fundamental breakthroughs in communications and IT came from Japan. Huge R&D programs are now being mounted in Japan to redress the situation, with research emphasis in the areas of new materials, superconductors (which are critical to Japan's program of mass-transit levitation vehicles) and artificial intelligence.

Software Enormous effort is also being expended in software development and training, where there is an acknowledged large gap between demand and supply. Unless these skills are accelerated there will be an estimated shortage of a million computer software specialists by the turn of the century.

Quality of life In contrast to Japan's high GNP per head, domestic living standards are low compared to most Western countries. Housing is cramped, generally of poor quality and, even in metropolitan areas, frequently unsewered—some 30% of homes in the Tokyo-Yokohama belt are not connected to public sewerage systems.

Urban infrastructure Other urban infrastructure systems are also underprovided. Roads are highly congested, with few exceptions, and an otherwise excellent train system is subject to heavy peak-hour overcrowding, with a substantial percentage of lines due for upgrading or replacement. Suburban electricity and telephone distributions are still almost entirely by overhead poles and wires.

Aging population The declining birth and mortality rates are resulting in an increasingly aging population. This is adding to the already pressing problems of support and care of the elderly, which in the past were supplied through the extended family. With changing family structure and social values, however, this support is fast becoming inadequate and new social infrastructures for the aged will need to be developed.

These problems are officially acknowledged and publicly documented but there are two other significant problem areas that are less often articulated. The first is the widening gap between corporate affluence and domestic austerity. While the reserves of the giant manufacturing companies and trading houses escalate into billions of dollars, the average Japanese family struggles against an inordinately high cost of living. Though wages and GNP per head are not far below the USA, the cost of essentials such as food, housing and transportation seems to be almost double that of the USA. Even the domestic prices of Japanese cameras and electronic appliances exceed their equivalent overseas prices. Recognition of the disparity between national economic wealth and personal purchasing power, compared to other countries, is not yet widespread but could become a source of political instability.

A second problem is a growing concern—at present limited to the more "internationalized" sector of the population—that Japan is perceived by the rest of the world as little more than a production powerhouse, making little contribution to solving the world's problems or to world culture. Although patently untrue by many measures—Japan ranks among leading nations in Third World aid and produces more than its fair share of symphony soloists and conductors—that collective view is disturbing to many in senior levels of government and commerce. As with all underlying insecurity, there is a need to be reassured and to feel wanted.

National goals and strategies

Japan's earlier national goals were essentially cast around economic development. Now that economic targets have been met, today's primary national goals are to:

Improve the quality of life of the Japanese people, through higher standards of housing, physical infrastructure and community services

Contribute to global political and economic stability, social development and world peace

Focus domestic economic development to support these goals.

The strategies for the achievement of these goals are as follows:

Transformation of industry along the spectrum from heavy to light, to information and knowledge-based industry.

Hence to become an "information society," with the information industry sector contributing over 25% of GNP by the year 2000.

Wide-ranging programs of urban redevelopment and renewal, upgrading the physical environment, living standards and services, and creating better informed societies. The present dominance of Tokyo-Yokohama and Osaka is to be redressed.

Internationalization. Development of new overseas markets, increased Third World aid, promotion of further overseas travel and tourism among Japanese—there already is a travel agent on the ground floor of almost every large office block in Tokyo—and import promotion.

Nationwide education programs in IT, hardware and software. Sponsoring of increased basic research in these areas.

Urban planning

Viewed against the backdrop of Japan's problems and professed national goals, the construction of "information cities"—whether by urban renewal or new cities programs—provides an almost perfect match to the implementation strategies outlined above. The one missing strategy is internationalization. But if information cities are promoted internationally and also built in other countries through intergovernment joint ventures (as proposed with the Japan-Australia multi-function polis discussed below) then the strategic match is complete.

As indicated above, massive and multiple urban development programs are well under way, the first phases of which center on urban planning and public relations. Public relations involves the marketing of urban development plans to the citizens who will live and work there and to the industries which will provide much of the finance for their own transformation, aided by central and municipal governments and the large financial institutions.

International workshop on information cities

The international workshop was jointly sponsored by the Japanese Association for Planning Administration (JAPA) and Massachusetts Institute of Technology's (MIT's) East Asian Architecture and Planning Program, with cooperation from the Tokyo Institute of Technology (Department of Social Engineering). It was hosted by and held in the cities of Kawasaki and Osaka, 1–26 August 1988. The 29 participants came from 14 countries and comprised roughly equal numbers of post-graduate students and practitioners in architecture, urban planning or communications.

The main test bed for the workshop was Kawasaki. It is a city of 1.3 million inhabitants, about 2 km wide and 20 km long, sandwiched between Tokyo and Yokohama and running alongside the Tama river. Now part of a continuous urban sprawl, it was once a main agricultural center and staging post on the old Edo (Tokyo)-Kyoto way.

Kawasaki: background history   Kawasaki has a long history of planning dating back to 1559 when an extensive "spine and vertebrae" canal system was constructed for irrigation and subsequently also used for transporting agricultural products. Today the canal system is largely disused except for some stormwater drainage and occasional recreation places. In the 20th century Kawasaki developed as a major industrial center and in 1960 the first metropolitan plan for heavy industry and a population of 1 million was produced. Today Kawasaki accounts for nearly 12% of Japan's total production.

Subsequent plans in 1969 and 1974 changed the focus to light industry and an increased population, with recognition of growing community needs. In 1981 the fourth metropolitan plan, "Kawasaki 2001," was produced. It focused heavily on community needs and services, an improved environment, citizen participation and supporting information access systems.

In 1986 twin concepts of Kawasaki—as an information city and as a city of knowledge-based industries—were fully merged in the plan for Kawasaki Campus City—a city of linked specialist areas, akin to a university campus. Eighteen centers of knowledge specialization, including government, education, arts, international relations, medical research, and so on, were nominated and are to be linked by high-capacity information highways. Central to this plan is the establishment of a new institution, the Kawasaki Institute of Technology (KIT), as a type of open university distributed over all the knowledge centers.

In developing a succession of municipal plans, Kawasaki aims to extract maximum benefit from the range of government national planning initiatives. The central city of Kawasaki also qualifies as a model future information metropolis under MITI's advanced information cities program, as well as a teletopia under MPT's program. Three urban zones are also nominated under the Ministry of Construction's intelligent cities programs.

In 1987 the Kawasaki municipality, in association with JAPA, announced an international competition for planning the future of Kawasaki as an information city. It attracted world-wide interest, receiving 200 entries from over 20 countries. Seven major prizes were awarded, including the grand prize which was won by Peter Droege, a US-based architect and planner, formerly on the staff of MIT.[5]

The competition brief had advanced the central theme of Kawasaki Campus City, characterized by information systems supporting a wide range of business, commercial, educational, social and leisure pursuits, and collectively comprising an "intelligent city." The entries showed an imaginative diversity in their approach and spawned a hierarchy of "intelligent" spaces and places, from central and neighborhood information plazas to information-access mobiles and "smart boxes" in streets, parks and shopping malls. Intelligent office buildings and dwellings housed a variety of linked systems monitoring environmental conditions and safety, controlling utility services and giving access to wide community information systems.

Intelligent buildings already constitute a high-growth industry in Japan. One showpiece is the Ark Hills center in downtown Tokyo. In addition to fully integrated, computer-controlled services and a standby generation plant that would support a medium-sized city, it also features the Himawari, or Sunflower, solar system in which sunlight is concentrated from huge, automatic tracking lens-arrays into optical fibers, and piped around the building for health and medical, fish breeding and indoor horticultural uses. The intelligent building concept, linked with office automation systems, is being strongly promoted by information industry leaders like Toshiba, NEC and Hitachi, and ranks high on new-product export agendas.

Workshop outcomes The workshop organized itself into three study groups:

Living environment, embracing housing, workplace and leisure

Museum, being a pseudonym for cultural, knowledge and informal education activities

City hall, representing the spectrum of government-citizen relationships.

Specific outcomes in terms of proposed urban forms were less significant to workshop participants than the process of trying to extract, from all the rhetoric, complexity and apparent confusion which surrounds Kawasaki urban planning, some useful answers to the following basic questions:

What are the underlying societal values and associated planning goals?

What is the real mechanism of progress toward these goals?

What function was the workshop intended to fulfill?

Out of the study group and collective debate there emerged fair consensus views on a number of these issues.

There was a healthy skepticism about the values implicit in "information cities," i.e., whether technology could provide solutions to what are essentially social problems.

High-profile government commitment to city IT was seen to be motivated more by industry strategy than by the goal of citizen enlightenment through "informatization."

IT could be both a centralizing and a decentralizing force. Hence there was a perceived need to safeguard against widening disparities in power groups and the creation of information élites, and to provide freedom of information access, consistent with individual rights of privacy, and "information free" zones as retreats.

It was agreed that IT should be applied to reinforce a "return to community" and a sense of identity within neighborhoods. (The "neighborhood office" described below gives an example.)

It was felt that the old canal system should be refurbished and become the focus of the city information system, as the conduit for high capacity (optical fiber) systems linking neighborhoods and city wards, and by providing recreational paths and spaces for people interaction.

Greater citizen involvement was seen as essential in planning the future Kawasaki information city.

The primary function of the workshop was not its direct contribution to Kawasaki's urban planning but rather, as with the international competition, as part of the internationalization and legitimization of Japan's information cities policy and programs.

The museum and city hall were not seen as discrete physical locations, but rather as having distributed functions, with fixed and mobile elements extending from central city plazas to individual neighborhoods and dwellings. Both were centered around the idea of citizens having interactive encounters with past knowledge, present realities and future possibilities, and providing action-learning experiences.

The "living environment" group explored the Kawasaki City form using the Japanese city scale relationships of the ward (around 100,000 persons), the *cho* (a small suburb of around 10,000), the *cho nai kai* (traditional neighborhood community of around 1,000), and the *tatami* (individual dwelling).

Work decentralization: the neighborhood office A key element among the workshop's proposals for the future development of Kawasaki as an information city was the concept of the "neighborhood office" (NO). Of the 1.1 million inhabitants of Kawasaki, some 240,000 commute to Tokyo to work each day, with an average traveling time exceeding 2.5 hours. Reduced commuting time is a high priority development need, which will only be partially met by decentralizing production and better transportation.

The decentralization of office work offers another approach. In general, working from home (the home-office concept) has only limited application due to problems of social isolation, domestic stress, and so on, as shown by trials in a number of countries. Nevertheless, for some professionals such as journalists, designers and architects, it can be an important, if only partial, alternative. In Japan, however, the unique domestic culture, limited space and noise problems would make working from home even more difficult on any widespread scale.

An alternative approach is the NO. Located within half a kilometer of the home with an access time of less than 10 minutes, it would cater to the needs of many types of office and information workers—that is, all those people who commute daily to cities in order to carry out what are essentially information transactions, such as reading and composing correspondence, referring to files, whether paper or computer-based, talking to individuals and being in conference, receiving and issuing directives, evaluating situations and making decisions. It is estimated that upwards of 100,000 Kawasaki commuters to Tokyo are in this category. Such people could, in principle, work from NOs, given an appropriate communications infrastructure and organization.

Each NO would cater to, typically, around 1,000 workers. This number can be varied to suit the local needs of the community and to strike the desired balance between minimum cost per worker (which favors larger groups), adequate socializing among the workers, for which reduced numbers might be preferred, and acceptable travel time. Larger groups reduce costs because they require less land-space per worker and less investment in transmission, access facilities and terminals.

A repertoire of modern telecommunications facilities would be available, with shared access to high-capacity information highways (optical fiber system) running as a spine through Kawasaki and linking through to Tokyo, where the highways would be subdivided and switched to the participating organization offices. These would initially be the larger organizations which have already automated their office systems.

In addition to screen-based and other terminal devices normally provided in modern central office locations, an NO for up to 1,000 workers could also require 200 FAX terminals; 200 speech and medium-speech data ISDN circuits; 200 data only, dedicated channels for remote database access, file updating, word processing, and so on; 50 personal picturephone (dial-up) services; and 10 wideband facilities—videoconference, CAD/CAM etc. Table 1 sets out approximate transmission requirements per NO.

Based on the above requirements, each optical fiber pair could support 20 NOs using 1 Gigabit transmission systems. Estimates indicate that the total telecommunications cost (terminals, transmission, switching and videoconference equipment) would not exceed $2,000 capital per worker for a system of 10 or more NOs. This does not include building costs, since local office accommodations would be far less expensive than the central Tokyo offices that they would replace; this allows for 20% of the Tokyo offices to be retained to accommodate, say, one day in five at headquarters. Also, no cost for land access for cables has been included, since the government owns the canals and railway easements which could be used. The

Table 1. Transmission requirements per NO.	Function	Transmission requirement (megabits per second)
	Speech and data	14
	Dedicated data	4
	Picturephone	4
	Wideband circuits	20
	Total	42

annual cost of the system, covering interest, depreciation and maintenance, would not exceed $600 per worker.

Assuming that 200 return trips to Tokyo are avoided each year and that each saves two hours travel time, then annual savings would be about $1,580 (see Table 2).

As well as the net (minimum) economic benefits of around $1,000 per worker per year, there are other important, non-quantifiable benefits. These include:

Reinforcement of local community identity. The socialization of commuters to Tokyo offices must center around common interests, notably sports, news and the company. In the NO all workers come from the same local community and socialization can center more on neighborhood interests, events and common community problems. This could do much to rejuvenate an identity with local community, as a balance to the present over-dominant image of the company.

Increased leisure time of at least eight hours per week.

Reduced personal stress.

Help in redressing the dominance of Tokyo with respect to other cities, which is a stated national objective. In the long term this would also be reflected in some narrowing of the immense disparity in land values.

While the economic benefits of the NO are convincing, there are some serious practical impediments to its implementation. Since facilities are shared, it would require cooperation between user organizations, some of whom may be in market competition with others. It may be seen as eroding company loyalty by having decentralized staff in a shared environment. It demands that participating organizations have well developed office automation systems capable of being accessed remotely and of delivering all the necessary information for successful decentralization of work. There are standards and security implications in operating over a common telecommunications system and, finally, it requires strong, creative leadership on the part of Kawasaki municipality or some "third party" entrepreneur to initiate and drive the project as a joint venture. Fortunately, with the deregulation environment in Japan, it should be possible to

Table 2. Annual savings per worker due to use of neighborhood office.

Allocation	Cost	Annual saving ($)
Fares	$65 per month	780
Time	$2 per hour	800
Total saving		1,580

negotiate the problems of ownership, shared use and network interconnection.

Technical integration of telecommunications The optical fiber spine through Kawasaki, linking NOs to organizations in Tokyo, would also provide for other information needs in Kawasaki's development—for example, it would link the 18 campus sites and provide core communications for proposed new city hall and museum functions.

Network relationships The NO concept would best be implemented by means of a shared, private network. The use of a network separate from the public telecommunications network is justified by several factors, listed below.

Cost savings Ownership of transmission facilities, as proposed in the joint venture organization, means that recurrent operating costs are independent of usage, while the volume of traffic will be sufficient to ensure effective utilization of capacity. Because the sources and destinations of traffic are known and limited in number, the switching system need provide for vastly reduced interconnected possibilities as compared to the public telephone network. Modern private automatic branch exchanges (PABXs) can adequately carry out the switching functions at both the NO and the participating Tokyo organization offices.

Security of information The private network must prevent open access from outside users, and must be effectively partitioned within itself, so that each participating organization operates independently of the others. The first requirement is met by barring access into the network from the public network; access from the private to the public network is permitted. The second requirement, of internal security, can be provided by digital PABXs, utilizing ISDN "D" channel facilities, or by personal card-control of terminal devices. The question of commercial security along with the shared system efficiency is an important one, which would need detailed study in any pilot system.

System relationships The relationship of the proposed NO system to the telephone network and the CTV network is illustrated in Figure 1. Relating the technical network structure to the various levels of the city scale structure, we can identify typical information needs at each scale level, and the services that could be provided to meet them.

Cho (10,000 persons) Co-located with the *cho* NO would be a com-

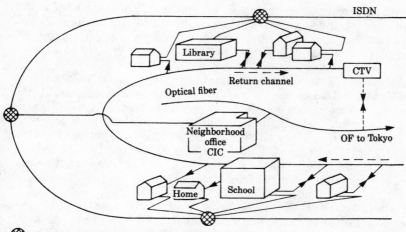

Public network telephone (ISDN) exchange
ISDN Integrated services digital network
CTV   Cable television network
OF   Optical fiber
CIC   Community information center

Figure 1. The neighborhood office: network relationships.

munity information center (CIC). Depending upon local environment this could be, for example, part of a common building, a separate building or an adjacent information plaza. Services provided would include:

Community information via videotext terminals and database access. Examples are library, health, medical and social services, recreational information, and bulletin board with notices of community meetings and activities.

Public videoconference to other community centers on the network; for example, competitive and recreational activities (quiz contests, debates, and so on) and for discussion of common issues such as transportation and schooling problems.

Interaction with special interest groups, for example, ethnic languages, specialist library, musical or artistic interests using sound and/or visual media.

Education; groups studying at the center would have collective access to specialist teachers at other locations backed by personal computer terminals, with programmed learning linkages to community schools and other learning centers.

With the exception of quality video, all these facilities could be provided over public or private network ISDN 64 kilobits channels, using combinations of audio (personal and conference), data, fax and graphics services.

Cho nai kai (1,000 persons)   Community information points would be strategically located in shopping centers, primary schools, libraries and other places where local residents regularly visit. These would provide for individual rather than group information access. Facilities could include videotext, fax, personal computer, and so on, as subsets of the *cho* CIC and could be supported by simple telephone circuits. Some of the services would be delivered to the community information point from that center.

Tatami (dwelling)   Home facilities could be the same as for the *cho nai kai*, but in practice would be constrained by the cost of home terminal equipment and the suitability of the home environment in terms of available space and noise levels. Individual family needs would vary widely, but experience so far suggests that working from home and the intelligent house have limited application in the foreseeable future. Notable exceptions include home and personal security systems which are now becoming more affordable, and supplementary home learning with access via personal computer.

Ward (100,000)   Moving upscale from the *cho* to the ward, the NO would probably incorporate additional facilities to meet the specialized needs of local government administration. This could mean an increase in the scale of services rather than the type, such as increased use of CAD/CAM for government and utility planning. In some wards which housed industry with high-profile international relations, a teleport with direct satellite access might be justified, for example, at an R&D park development. As joint owner in the total NO system, the city could utilize its private network capacity for government business with Tokyo. This would include government information exchange with central bodies such as MITI, MTP, the Ministry of Construction and the Treasury. Conferencing and large-scale document interchange could be carried out over the high-capacity media.

Hidden agendas?

Personal evaluation of the underlying purpose and importance of Japan's information cities program was continually reshaped as the workshop revealed successive layers incorporated in the planning process.

Initial impressions of the Japanese government's grand design, lofty social goals and enormous resources were soon tempered by an awareness of conflict and poor coordination between the agencies, and by the realization that technology cannot provide instant solutions to essentially human problems. Exposure to information city projects being implemented showed that, despite the rhetoric, priorities were dominated by commercial rather than social goals.

Realization then emerged that the underlying primary goal was not citizen informatization, but rather the long-term restructuring of Japan's production capacity toward ITs and knowledge industries. The idea of information cities provides a tangible rallying point, incentive and test bed for the advancement of a wide range of IT applications (both hardware and software). These include wideband services, optical fiber systems, office automation, intelligent buildings and transport systems, high definition video and cable TV, which all have high export and domestic potential. Finally, there is the paradox that information cities could make the achievement of certain social goals a self-fulfilling prophecy. Hence, in the process of legitimizing national economic goals, it becomes vital to gain widespread Japanese acceptance of the social goals of information cities.

International implications of the multi-function polis (MFP)

The match between information cities and national goals becomes complete with recent Japanese proposals to establish such cities abroad, based around joint ventures with selected country governments whose economies would benefit by large capital inflow. Such proposals meet Japan's criteria in helping to redress its foreign exchange imbalance, establish new overseas manufacture and create desirable overseas environments for Japanese research and tourism, tailored to specific needs.

One such proposal was made to the Australian government in 1986 through MITI, for a multi-function polis to be constructed as a joint undertaking. It was to be a city "of the fifth space," combining in the one location the requirements of the four spaces—dwelling, workplace, entertainment and "retreat." It was to be a knowledge-based, high-technology city built in a site of natural beauty and developed in harmony with the environment. It would be international, with centers of advanced learning and research and a limited population (less than 150,000), at least half of which would be transient, remaining for periods varying from holidays of a few weeks to postings of a few years. It would rely heavily on advanced information and communications technologies to support local services and to provide instant access between research and academic institutions—linking databases world-wide—and between the city's international population and its overseas communities of interest.

Five of the six states in Australia started to develop proposals to win selection as the MFP site and the federal government soon faced a sensitive political dilemma in having to make the decision, since the Japanese government felt that this was outside its legitimate domain. Realizing the political ramifications, the federal government appears to have taken the course of trying to develop a new concept of a "decentralized MFP," which would draw on the best compatible features of the states' proposals. It could be argued that with advanced communications, notably telecommunications, physical proximity is of less importance. On the other hand there is no denying the fact that many of the attributes originally sought—proximity of all the four "spaces," harmonious development in a natural environment, as well as physical identity—would have to be foregone.

It will be interesting to see whether such a marked change of course will be acceptable to the Japanese government. If social and cultural values dominate the Japanese conception, then it would be hard to support a decentralized MFP. However, if, as the information cities experience suggests, Japan's dominant motive is information industry development, then the effective decimation of the original MFP concept, far from sabotaging it, could actually reinforce it because of the new information flows needed between its widespread, decentralized parts. It would be even more advantageous for Japan if a Japanese telecommunications carrier were permitted to operate those "intra-city" services. While such a role would be inadmissible in the present regulatory environment, it could become a reality in a negotiated MFP joint venture between the two governments, some few years in the future.

1. W. H. Dutton, J. G. Blumler and K. L. Kraemer, "Continuity and Change in Conceptions of the Wired City," in *Wired Cities* (G. K. Hall, 1986); W. H. Dutton, "Wired Cities and Nations: A Perspective on Future Developments in Telecommunications," paper presented at the IRIS Conference, 1984.
2. M. Kawahata, "HI-OVIS," in *Wired Cities*.
3. F. Gerin and X. deTavernost, "Biarritz and the Future of Videocommunications," in *Wired Cities*.
4. E. White, "Recent Pilot Cable Projects," in *Wired Cities*.
5. P. Droege, "Japan's Advanced Information Cities" and other papers, *Places: Journal of Environmental Design 5* (3), 1988.

Class of 2000: The Good News and the Bad News

— Marvin J. Cetron

The high-school graduating class of 2000 is with us already; its members entered kindergarten in September 1987. The best of them are bright, inquiring, and blessed with all the benefits that caring, attentive parents can provide. They will need all those advantages and more. The class of 2000, and their schools, face educational demands far beyond those of their parents' generation. And unless they can meet those demands successfully, the United States could be nearing its last days as a world power.

No one had to tell Ben Franklin or Thomas Jefferson that their new country would live or die with its school system. In a democracy, citizens must be able to read, so they can learn about the issues on which they are voting. (No, television and radio have not made reading unnecessary.) They must know history so that they can develop political judgments and not be taken in by the false promises of unscrupulous candidates. Today, they must also understand basic science so that they can make informed decisions about such issues as the space program, nuclear power, computer technology, and genetic engineering.

Preparing for 2000

The class of 2000 will need a far better education simply to get a decent job. In part, this is because today's fast-growing employment areas—the ones where good jobs can be found—are fields such as computer programming, health care, and law. They require not only a high-school diploma, but advanced schooling or job-specific training.

Reprinted, with permission, from THE FUTURIST, published by the World Future Society, 4916 Saint Elmo Avenue, Bethesda, Maryland 20814.

By contrast, less than 6% of workers will find a place on the assembly lines that once gave high-school graduates a good income; the rest will have been replaced by robots. Instead, service jobs will form nearly 90% of the economy. A decade ago, about 77% of jobs involved at least some time spent in generating, processing, retrieving, or distributing information. By the year 2000, that figure will be 95%, and that information processing will be heavily computerized.

Traditional jobs also call for more familiarity with technology; even a department store sales clerk must be "computer literate" enough to use a computerized inventory system. Approximately 60% of today's jobs are open to applicants with a high-school diploma; among new jobs, more than half require at least some college. By the year 2010, virtually every job in the country will require some skill with information-processing technology.

Beyond that, simply living in modern society will raise the level of education we all need. By the year 2000, new technology will be changing our working lives so fast that we will need constant retraining, either to keep our existing jobs or to find new ones. Even today, engineers find that half of their professional knowledge is obsolete within five years and must go back to school to keep up; the rest of us will soon join them in the classroom. Knowledge itself will double not once, not twice, but four times by the year 2000! In that single year, the class of 2000 will be exposed to more information and knowledge than their grandparents experienced in a lifetime.

The challenge for schools

Schools will have to meet these new demands. Today, schools offer adult education as a community service or in hope of earning sorely needed revenue. In the future, they will be teaching adults because they haven't any choice. Many public schools will be open 24 hours a day, retraining adults from 4 p.m. to midnight and renting out their costly computer and communications systems to local businesses during the graveyard shift.

Fortunately, American schools can provide top-quality education when they make the effort to do so. The proof can be seen not only in affluent suburbs, but in some cities. In Fairfax, a community of about 350,000, Mantua Elementary School principal Joe Ross has made this effort. His "school for all reasons, school for all seasons" seems quite ordinary on the outside. But enter its tiled halls and you will find yourself surrounded by multicolored posters depicting cultural highlights of Kuwait—all written in Arabic. Other posters appear in languages ranging from German to Vietnamese—and all are readily understood by children who are eight or nine years old. Children learn sign language as early as kindergarten, when basic consonants are taught. The school is stocked with desktop computers, and there is video equipment for every room.

Specialized classes are a major feature of Mantua's educational program. There are classrooms filled with high-technology devices to aid handicapped students. Advanced students hone their thinking skills in programs designed for the gifted and talented. At one end of the building, a school-age–child-care center continues the educational process long after traditional school hours have ended. There are also programs for the hearing impaired, the learning disabled, preschool handicapped, and English as a Second Language students.

Mantua's educational system works. Its average students rank far higher than the national average, and all the specialized programs manage to extract top grades from students who in many cases might be expected to fail. Perhaps more importantly, the Mantua Elementary children are exposed to and work with the students in the special programs mentioned above and know they are an integral part of a pluralistic society. These children will better accept each person, whatever his or her gift or handicap, as an individual and not as someone to be stared at.

Parental guidance suggested

Parental involvement is the key to making the system work. At Mantua, teachers have long emphasized this need. According to my wife, Gloria, who teaches kindergarten at the school, it is very simple: "When the parents get involved, the kids do better." In an effort to get the parents involved, Gloria and her aide, Lynn Curran, asked parents of the kindergartners in the class of 2000 what they are doing to prepare their children for the year 2000. Jason Hovell's parents answered, "To prepare a child for the year 2000, we think a child needs a first-rate education and strong family relationships." The parents of Sarah Crutchfield believe that "exposing [her] to the avenues of learning . . . [through] library trips, museums, nature walks, and the theater" will be the best preparation.

Many of the parents expressed concern about the moral fabric of America. Heather Goodwin's parents are "trying to rear her in a manner that leads to upright moral conduct and ethical practices, to teach her to believe in herself and stand up for what is right, and to respect the views and beliefs of others." The parents go to the head of the class. They are at the first critical stage of awareness.

The state of education today

Programs similar to those at Mantua Elementary are available—and successful—all over the country. Unfortunately, these remain rare bright spots in a bleak educational picture. There is all too much evidence that American schools are failing many students. In 1982, American eighth-graders taking a standardized math test answered only 46% of the questions correctly, which put them in the bottom half of the 11 nations participating. (Japanese children got

64% correct.) That same year, the top 5% of twelfth-graders from nine developed countries, the ones who had taken advanced math courses, took standardized tests of algebra and calculus. America's best and brightest came in dead last.

The failure is not limited to tough subjects like math. Other studies have shown that only one high-school junior in five can write a comprehensible note applying for a summer job; that among high-school seniors, fewer than one-third know to within 50 years when the Civil War took place, and one in three does not know that Columbus discovered America before 1750.

More than 500,000 children drop out of school each year; in some school districts, the dropout rate exceeds 50%. Perhaps 700,000 more students in each class finish out their 12 years hardly able to read their own diplomas. Among young adults, one government-sponsored study found, well under 40% can understand an average *New York Times* article or figure out their change when paying for lunch, and only 20% have mastered the weighty intellectual challenge of reading a bus schedule.

The results of this endemic ignorance can already be seen throughout American society. The sad condition of America's once-great space program is a heartrending comment on the state of science education in the country; as a nation, we simply are not qualified to manage large, demanding technological problems. And listen to the National Restaurant Association, which estimates that by the year 1995 a million jobs in their industry will go unfilled because too many entry-level job hunters are too poorly educated to succeed even as waiters, cashiers, and hamburger flippers. By the year 2000, according to one estimate, the literacy rate in America will be only 30%.

Training for the future

Solving the problems of conventional education is only one half of the task. America will also need a much stronger system of vocational education if it is to meet the challenge of the years to come. On average, the next generation of workers will have to make no fewer than five complete job changes in a lifetime, not counting the multiple tasks (which will also be changing) associated with each respective job. This is a mandate for continuous retraining.

In the future, vocational training will be just as crucial as traditional education. If schools fail to turn out well-educated high-school and college graduates, more and more young people will find themselves unqualified for any meaningful career, while millions of jobs go begging for trained people to fill them. If schools and businesses fail to retrain adults for the growing technical demands of their jobs, millions of conscientious workers will find their careers cut short, and the skilled work they should have done will be exported to countries like Japan and Taiwan, where educational systems definitely are up to the task.

Education for the class of 2000

America's school system today is clearly overburdened, even by the traditional demands placed on it. How can the school system be strengthened to bring high-quality education to all members of the class of 2000? And what can be done about the growing demand for adult education in the years to come? Over half a dozen measures come to mind, most of them embarrassingly simple:

Lengthen the school day and year   In any field, you can get more work done in eight hours than in six, in 10 days than in seven. Japan's school year consists of 240 eight-hour days. America's averages 180 days of about 6.5 hours. So let's split the difference: Give us 210 seven-hour school days a year.

Cut the median class size down from 17.8 to 10 students   Naturally, this means hiring more teachers. This will give teachers more time to focus on the *average* student.

Not too long ago, schools were just beginning to recognize the needs of special students with learning disabilities or exceptional talents. Now there are programs for the learning disabled and the gifted and talented, as there should be. But, in focusing attention and resources on the needs of the minority at the extremes, the nation's schools have neglected the needs of the majority in the middle. American students' dismal performance on standardized tests attests to this.

Inadequate attention at school is exacerbated by inadequate attention at home for the average student. The big advantage that schools like Mantua enjoy over less-successful institutions is not their specialized programs, but the fact that their students are drawn largely from traditional families where parents are available and are actively interested in the child's education. Where one-parent homes are the rule, teachers must provide the individual attention that parents cannot. In crowded classrooms, they simply can't do it. The answer is to cut class size.

Computerize   Computer-aided learning programs are already replacing drill books; as software improves, they will begin to replace some kinds of textbooks as well. More teachers should be actively involved in writing the software. The best computerized learning programs already include primitive forms of artificial intelligence that can diagnose the student's learning problems and tailor instruction to compensate for them.

"We can put 30 computers in a room, and they will go as fast or as slow as each child needs; the child controls it," observes Representative James Scheuer (Democrat, New York). "He has an equal and comfortable relationship, building his morale and self-esteem, which can only enhance the learning process."

The result may not be as good as having highly skilled, caring teachers give hours of personal attention to each student, but computerization is a lot easier to achieve, and it's a big improvement over today's situation. This should be an easy notion to sell to taxpayers; in a survey of parents of Mantua kindergartners, fully two-thirds cited computers as one of the most important topics their children should learn in school.

But making this transition won't be cheap. By 1990, the United States will already have spent $1 billion on computerized learning, but two-thirds of that will have been spent by affluent parents for their own children. If public school systems fail to develop their own programs, the less-affluent students could suffer an irreparable educational disadvantage.

Tailor courses to the needs of individual students Individualized education programs (IEPs) are already used in many schools; they suggest which skills the student should practice and recommend ways of testing to make sure they have been learned. But far more is possible.

In the future, IEPs will look at the student's learning style: whether they learn best in small groups or large classes; whether they learn best from reading, lectures, or computer programs; how much supervision they need; and so on. Teachers will be evaluated in the same way and assigned to large or small classes, good readers or good listeners, as best suits them. These programs may not be adopted in time to help the class of 2000, but the sooner the better.

Promote students based on performance, not on time served in class Students starting school in 2000 will move up not by conventional grade levels, but by development levels, ensuring that each child can work on each topic until it's mastered.

Recruit teachers from business and industry, not just university educational programs Get chemists to teach chemistry, accountants to teach arithmetic, and so on. These specialists could become teachers in areas where teachers are scarce. Give them the required courses in education necessary to meet teaching standards. But start by making sure that would-be teachers actually know something worth teaching.

Set new priorities for school systems that today are overregulated and underaccountable In many communities, the curriculum is so standardized that teachers in any given course on any given day will be covering the same material. It's time to cut through that kind of red tape and give teachers the right to do the job they supposedly were trained for. Then make teachers and their supervisors responsible for the performance of their students. Teachers who turn out well-educated students should be paid and promoted accordingly. If students don't advance, neither should their would-be educators.

Bring business and industry into the public school system   Corporations must train and retrain workers constantly, and that requirement will grow ever more pressing. The obvious answer is for them to contract with schools to do the teaching. The money earned from such services can go toward teachers' salaries and investments in computers, software, and such things as air conditioning needed to keep schools open all year.

For students not headed toward college, businesses may also provide internships that give high-school students practical experience in the working world they are about to enter. When public schools turn out graduates who haven't mastered reading, writing, or math, business suffers.

Finally, if Americans really want quality education, they must be willing to pay for it   Since 1984, the White House has attempted to cut the national education budget by more than $10 billion. Though Congress has always restored most of those proposed cuts, the federal government actually spent, after inflation, about 14% less for education in 1988 than it did five years earlier.

Teachers are still dramatically underpaid compared with other professions that require a college education. In 1987, the average starting salary for an accountant was $21,200, new computer specialists received $26,170, and engineers began at $28,500. The average starting salary for teachers was only $17,500.

Today's education system cannot begin to prepare students for the world they will enter on graduation from high school. By 2030, when the class of 2000 will still be working, they will have had to assimilate more inventions and more new information than have appeared in the last 150 years. By 2010, there will be hardly a job in the country that does not require skill in using powerful computers and telecommunications systems.

America needs to enact all the reforms outlined above, and many others as well. It is up to concerned citizens, parents, and teachers to equip our children with the knowledge and skills necessary to survive and thrive in the twenty-first century.

Back to Basics

Marj Charlier

What do you do with bank tellers whose arithmetic is lousy, production workers who can't read work-order changes, employees of all kinds whose basic knowledge level is so low that they can't do their jobs well? You open a little red schoolhouse in your plant or office and you do the work of the school system all over again. This goes by the fancy name of remediation, and if you do it right you get graduates like Dorothy Watson.

Eight years ago Ms. Watson, a black single mother who is now 40, appeared to have a limited future in the high-tech workplace, if she had one at all. Though she'd been the first of her 15 siblings to complete high school, she couldn't remember how to add and subtract fractions and she never had learned how to convert inches to centimeters. She'd never taken algebra, chemistry or physics.

Today, after in-house courses in math and science provided by her employer, Polaroid Corp., she uses what she's learned to tell a computer-controlled machine in a microelectronics lab how to slice silicon wafers for lasers. Besides math, she has gotten interested in chemistry and refers knowledgeably to isotopes, polarity and radicals. She is at home in a new kind of American workplace where so many others do not fit.

Triple whammy

It didn't used to matter that they didn't fit; the potential work force was large enough to allow companies to cherry-pick the more capable applicants and leave the rest. But now a worker shortage looms, part of a triple whammy that is threatening American competitiveness across the board, and companies are rapidly being forced into remediation programs to escape its effects.

As the huge baby-boom generation gives way to that of the baby bust, companies can no longer be picky in hiring. "Employers who used to cream the most qualified from an oversized labor pool increasingly will have to make rather than buy skilled employees," says a study by the American Society of Training and Development (ASTD).

At the same time, jobs are becoming ever more complex and demanding of higher skill levels—while the crisis in education is producing potential workers less and less able to do even today's work, much less tomorrow's.

An estimated 23 million Americans are functionally illiterate, meaning that their reading and computational skills are very low. Some experts estimate that up to 65% of the work force is "intermediately" literate, meaning that this group can read at between fifth-grade and ninth-grade levels. "That just isn't going to cut it when most workplace materials are written on the 12th-grade level," says Michael Higgins, president of Cox Educational Services, a consulting firm in Dallas.

This adds up to a tremendous need for remediation—a need that American industry has been slow to recognize. Though the $30 billion it spends on formal training of all kinds seems respectable, that sum still only amounts to 1.5% of total payroll and involves only 10% of the work force. Furthermore, much of the money is spent not on basic skills instruction for workers but on training for managers.

Signs of change

There are signs that this is changing. The ASTD says that 70% of the Fortune 500 companies it surveyed plan to spend more on education and training this year. New remediation programs are popping up at many companies, joining those already in place at such companies as Polaroid, Aetna Life & Casualty Co., Ford Motor Co., Control Data Corp., Motorola Inc., and many others.

Industry groups are weighing in, too. Simon & Schuster's new Workplace Resources Division is developing a program for the American Bankers Association that would train financial-services employees in basic reading and math skills. And the National Association of Printers and Lithographers is working up a variety of instructional plans for printers after 63% of its members said in a survey that they had had "negative results"—equipment failure, spoiled paper or misuse of chemicals—because of basic educational deficiencies among workers.

An increasing emphasis on quality, seen as necessary if U.S. companies are to compete in a global economy, is prompting more remediation efforts. Texas Instruments Inc., for example, started its first such program in 1989 at a plant that was suffering a high rate of job defects; the company found that needed work-order changes weren't being properly made because too many workers couldn't read well enough or interpret blueprints correctly.

Although it's too soon to measure the effects on work quality, program coordinator Wayne Freeland is encouraged by the feedback he's getting from employees. "They tell us about personal things," he says, "like how they're able to read to their grandchildren. One man said he can read billboards for the first time."

Remediation programs are often adopted in tandem with major changes in process, such as computer-integrated manufacturing, that demand more responsibility and more literacy of workers. "Industries didn't know they had basic-skills problems until they became automated," says Carl Haigler of the Mississippi governor's literacy office.

Rapid growth in a thin labor market can make remediation a painful necessity, as Peavey Electronics Corp., based in Meridian, Miss., discovered. Peavey, a well-known maker of electric guitars and amplifiers, has been on a hiring binge, adding 264 jobs in the past year to a work force that now stands at 1,900. There were slim pickings in the eastern Mississippi area—"We're just tapping out the resources," says Vice President Melinda Peavey—and the company had to settle for many new workers lacking the educational tools to handle much more than the simplest work.

To upgrade them, Peavey volunteered to test a federal plan that adapts the U.S. Army's Job Skills Education Program to a corporate setting. Computers are used to teach employees up to 300 things, including basic subjects such as math, as well as specific skills such as reading graphs and interpreting blueprints and schematic drawings. Every job in the plant is being analyzed, and the curricula for worker-students are being based on what each employee needs to know to do a particular job well.

Peavey's ultimate goal is to prepare employees for more demanding, technical jobs. Currently, workers in Peavey's assembly plants put components together with the guidance of pictures. But component configurations can change almost daily, and Ms. Peavey wants employees who can punch up work changes on a computer and teach themselves to change the assemblies. "I want those picture guides off the floors," she says.

The company is pleased with progress to date. Since September, when 64 employees began taking 40 hours of classroom instruction on company time, supervisors say they have noticed an improvement in productivity.

Quantifying it, of course, is difficult. But pretty much everyone agrees on this much: Improving worker literacy can't help but improve results, even if no one can be sure by how much. That is certainly an article of faith at Boston-based Polaroid, which started its first remediation effort 30 years ago. Today, under its Technology Readiness program, it has 800 of its 8,000 workers taking classes—on company time and at full pay—at any given time.

Employees who sign up are tested to determine what grade level they belong in. When they complete courses, they are certified as being qualified to do certain jobs requiring a certain level of knowledge and skill. The instruction is tied to work; students bring factory-floor problems to class, and reading teachers use flashcards that match words with camera parts the students assemble on the job.

Specific departments can request and get classes tailored to certain jobs. Manager Denis Murphy, for example, found that while workers in his lens laboratory could learn to handle a single work-station operation, they failed when asked to switch to a different one; they couldn't read the operating instructions, it turned out. Since 75 of them began custom-tailored classes 2½ years ago, productivity has climbed and workers have become more versatile. "We don't see the same trauma every Monday morning when they face a new machine," says Mr. Murphy.

Currently, the Tech Readiness staff is remediating 200 employees, temporary workers whom the company wants to upgrade and hire as permanent workers, in a three-year program at one camera factory. The employees are mostly Portuguese, Creole and Italian-speaking immigrants. About 15% of them couldn't read or write in any language, and many had never been inside a school. All needed training to bring their reading and math skills up to the level required to program manufacturing robots. They're getting it now.

In this instance, Polaroid could have filled the permanent job slots with better-qualified applicants. But Acquanetta Farrell, director of the Tech Readiness program, knows that Polaroid—and industry in general—will have to cope not only with a smaller labor pool but one containing a sharply higher proportion of minorities and immigrants, people likely to be even more lacking in education than others.

Learning how to upgrade them, then, is not only desirable but also necessary. "We can't just continue to buy technology and think that will make our work better," she says. "We have to develop people, too."

The remediation programs at Polaroid are popular with employees. Ed Coughlan, who manages a plant in Norwood, Mass., heard a worker on the floor berating a colleague who had to take a class again because he hadn't studied. "That's my seat you're taking," the worker said. Employees who take classes often show a marked increase in confidence, breadth of interests, and enthusiasm, and some become salesmen for the program within the company.

Robert Dunn is one of them. A co-worker of Dorothy Watson, he was the one who inspired her to take the classes that led to her present high-tech job in microelectronics and that have given her a deepening interest in science.

Mr. Dunn, a 44-year-old high-school dropout, is a Polaroid reclamation project himself. He started taking company-sponsored classes in 1979; by 1987 he had earned his high-school diploma and turned himself into something of a mathematics whiz (he would post algebra problems on a break-room blackboard to see whether anyone could solve them). Recently, he designed a device that measures the time it takes for material to pass between two rollers and that passes the information along to a computer. Now he's taking calculus.

Mr. Dunn, who never got past the ninth grade, is particularly happy that his 18-year-old daughter has decided to go to college. He says proudly: "I think it's primarily because she's seen what I've done."

Training and Education: The Competitive Edge

Jeffrey Hallett

If there was ever an issue that defined the crux of the challenge America faces over the next decade, it is that of training and education. Perhaps spoiled by several generations of economic success and world leadership, we have lost the sense of urgency and importance we once assigned to our educational systems. More importantly, as we now turn to remedy the situation, we must craft programs and methods that address the needs of students and employees in a new economy.

There are three pivotal factors that will determine the success or failure of any effort to improve training and education. First, the goals must be clear. The question of "training and education for what?" must be answered, agreed upon and communicated to all involved.

Second, we must determine if education and training should be treated as an expense or an investment. Our level of effort and the measurement of results will depend on this answer. Finally, we must assign responsibility for leadership, delivery and results.

Even before addressing these factors, however, we must evaluate the overall environment within which we are now working and competing. The relative importance of training and education within the current competitive context must be determined. Without this first step, we will be unable to make the best possible resource allocation decisions.

This is no simple task at any level. As a nation, for instance, we have to determine whether the nation is better served through additional investments in defense, agricultural subsidies, health care or

Reprinted with permission from HRMagazine (formerly Personnel Administrator), published by the Society for Human Resource Management, Alexandria, VA.

education and training. At the organizational level, we have to allocate funds to plant and equipment, advertising or training. At the individual level, we have to decide whether to spend precious money and time in additional training or take a vacation or buy a car, etc.

There are powerful arguments for making education and training the first priority. Many of the reasons are obvious. We have a shrinking pool of new workers, all tasks are requiring increasing levels of technical skill, and everything is in a constant state of flux. To remain competitive, our work force must have the knowledge, information and skills that allow us to maximize the use of new technology, that stimulate creativity and that allow us to achieve higher levels of productivity and quality at all levels of activity.

We are in an information-intensive, knowledge-based global economy. Organizations are discovering and announcing that "human resources are our most important asset." The catchwords of management are "excellence, quality, innovation, flexibility, being close to the customer," etc. To build these organizational characteristics, we keep experimenting with various forms of employee participation, decentralization, quality circles, quality of worklife programs, etc., to place a decision-making and authority closer to the action.

At the same time, business is discovering the direct relationship between the quality of the output of the educational system and the pool of available human resources. A series of blue-ribbon panels has declared that our educational system, once the envy of the world, has fallen behind other nations. A major segment of the population is effectively disenfranchised as 40 percent, 50 percent and more of our minority children are dropping out of school at early ages. Now that this population represents a growing proportion of the available work force over the next decade, we are beginning to pay some attention.

And paying attention is important, at least in the eyes of some competitors, as stated by Konosuke Matsushita of Matsushita Electric Industrial Co. in a 1979 speech: "Because we have measured better than you the scope of the new technological and economic challenges, we know that a handful of technocrats, no matter how brilliant and smart they might be, are no longer enough to create a real chance of success. Only by drawing on the combined brainpower of all its employees can a firm face up to the turbulence and constraints of today's environment.

"This is why large firms give their employees three to four times more training than yours. This is why they foster within the firm such intensive exchange and communications. This is why they constantly seek everyone's suggestions and why they demand from the educational system increasing numbers of specialists as well as bright and well-educated generalists, because these people are the lifeblood of industry."

The rate of change has accelerated to the point where the skills needed for any particular job change almost overnight. Computers, telecommunications, expert systems, robotics, computer-integrated manufacturing, bioengineering, holography, lasers, and other developments converge to create a world of explosive new opportunity and equally explosive potential for instantaneous obsolescence.

In this environment education and training are obviously important. The response, however, is not simply to patch the existing systems, allocate more resources to them, or bring higher levels of pay and respect to teachers. We are in a new economy and we need a new approach to education and training that is directed toward the demands of this new time.

This brings us to the question of "education and training for what?" The answer is simple—"to prepare individuals as fully as possible to contribute to their maximum potential within the current and future economy." This may be too obvious, but we must be certain that we are not moving in a direction that provides people with the skills and knowledge necessary to contribute to the industries, professions and organizations of the 1950s.

Too much of the nation's response to a growing recognition that our educational system has been failing, has been the attempt to return it to its state of excellence of several decades ago. "Back to basics" is a terrible theme and strategy. Back to the "good old days" is an alluring concept but an irresponsible approach to a serious problem. We need to go forward; we need to be clear about the needs of tomorrow and for the year 2000 and work to develop programs, policies and concepts that will best prepare us to be productive in these times.

This means that we have to be prepared to change everything about education and training. This requires a reexamination of how, when, to whom, where, and at whose cost training and education take place. The issue is not one of trying to fix our existing systems. The issue is the creation of the best educational and training opportunities we can imagine—regardless of their impact on existing institutions, traditions and programs.

Lifelong learning

A basic step we must now take is to recognize and celebrate the fact that education and learning must be pursued continuously throughout our lives. Elementary, secondary, post-secondary, graduate and post-graduate education are comfortable designations of a linear process designed for times of gradual change and for preparation for a "career" in a linear, batch-processing environment. This approach to education evolved during periods when information and knowledge were relatively fixed. Education was designed to advance people along "levels" of knowledge tightly bound with age and experience. Once through with our "education," we went on to "work" and then "retirement."

Change is so rapid today that what an individual learned five years ago is apt to be irrelevant. Scientific knowledge is exploding on all fronts, technical fields are in constant change, markets and industries are shifting at an increasing pace. And, most importantly, the best information about these changes is new and is not necessarily in the hands of traditional education and training institutions or a part of a prescriptive curriculum leading to a degree somewhere.

To construct a training and education environment that makes sense for these times requires that it be "ageless." It must overtly include training and educational opportunities for people of all ages. The environment must accommodate continuing movement in and out of the work force, and it must not be "wall-bound." Schools without walls must be reconstituted as learning without boundaries.

The technology of today and tomorrow accommodates all needs. With computers, telecommunications and videos, walls become irrelevant. Information can be transmitted anywhere, anytime at the speed of light. Increasingly, this information can be delivered interactively, with the individual learner determining the progress of the learning.

This, of course, undermines the social and political dynamics of education and training in the society. It democratizes access to information and knowledge and puts control directly in the hands of the consumer. It wreaks havoc with the whole structure of prerequisites and age.

A 12-year-old or a 60-year-old can and should have the opportunity to participate in a training program with the only requirement being their interest, determination and ability to complete the training. What should be important is maximization of the spread of information and knowledge. The primary determinant should be perceived needs and interests of individuals—wherever and whoever they might be.

Training on demand

Training on demand is needed within every organization. The issue is not the training programs, it is the training capacity. The investment to make is not in materials but in people. The training department, like the educational system, has to move to become a facilitator, a resource center, an aggressive seeker of new knowledge and new mechanisms for making that information available.

The private sector is not thrilled by the growing need to conduct remedial training programs for its work force. It looks at the demographic realities of the coming decade and clamors for a more effective school system. It also looks at the reality of constant change throughout the organization and at the need for more training just to stay competitive. Now, plant-closing laws will require companies to do more training of employees who are actually leaving the company.

From remedial English and basic math to the latest techniques of robotics or telecommunications or targeted marketing, the list of skills and areas of knowledge that the organization may have to deliver to its employees can seem endless and expensive. If, however, the training effort is one that is designed to meet the evolving needs of employees, whatever they might be, a course in algebra is as important and relevant as a course in advanced manufacturing techniques.

Why does this make sense? For starters, it makes sense because well-trained people do better jobs than those who are not trained. It makes sense because people who are well-trained have a better sense of self-worth and competence than most who are not. It makes sense because those who are given the opportunity to learn and be competent have a better sense of loyalty to their organization than those who are not given the opportunity.

At the results end we need excellence, innovation, productivity and high-quality customer relations. At the input end we need to reduce the costs of recruitment, of turnover, of absenteeism, of poor performance, etc. A commitment to training and education impacts all of these.

An open-ended opportunity

If we want a high-performance organization we must have high-performance people. We have to invest in these people on a continuous basis, and investment has to extend from the technical skills they need to the expansion of their capacity to learn through broader educational experiences. This type of training is still referred to as "soft-skill" and includes team building, negotiating, listening, stress management and time management.

Most human resource departments still find it difficult to squeeze the "soft-skill" training opportunities into their budgets unless the CEO happens to be personally committed to their value. If not, these are things that go first in a budget squeeze—right when they reflect precisely the skills needed to create and sustain a high-performance organization in turbulent times.

And training investments are now not just for the big boys or the high-tech companies. Training and education investments will make the difference in all organizations, particularly those that have traditionally not needed them. There have recently been dramatic examples of the effect on turnover—and therefore costs—in bakeries, retailing and printing operations—to say nothing of the success at Domino's Pizza, where training is an integral part of the company's strategy.

How? The best way to meet a learning or skill goal is as varied as the imagination. Successful training is not limited to the classroom. It often takes the form of a game or a simulation. Citicorp has a game it is developing to teach the subtle but seriously important issues of corporate ethics.

"Outward Bound" experiences have been highly endorsed by a large number of companies as critical to their success in building work groups that can really work well together. Summer sessions of advanced management courses at business schools bring new energy and excitement to many executives, while ongoing relationships between community colleges and local companies are driving the bulk of the new initiatives in training and education across the country.

Another critical aspect of maximizing the resources of the country and of the organization when addressing current and future training needs is the ability to draw upon talent and expertise wherever it exists. Again, this may appear to be a non-issue, but it is a large issue.

As we race into the age of computers and other related technologies, and as change continues to occur, we will find that those who know most about these things are YOUNG—to say nothing of being uncredentialed. This bothers our sense of the way things are "supposed to be."

Younger people are not supposed to be in a position of having more skills and knowledge than those who are older, more experienced and placed much higher in the organizational and social pecking order.

In our public schools, for example, we are really stuck for teachers to teach computing or programming. Teachers are too old; that is, they grew up before the computer revolution. It is the kids who have computing in their blood. Every school in the country has a cadre of young computer jocks who have grown up with computers and need no school-based training. They could teach other kids, they could even teach teachers and parents. They might need some assistance in the process of transmitting their knowledge, but they have the insights and skills necessary to assist others. Try suggesting this to a school board; then run for cover.

The same thing is true inside of organizations. A host of people scattered throughout all organizations have become computer literate, and they are not all in data processing or management information systems. Sooner or later they become the informal teachers, but they are rarely assembled as a resource and actively used to get others engaged because they do not have the status, the position or the age necessary to make this acceptable.

Knowledge = results

The fundamental need is to accept training and education as the primary objective of the organization and to focus on outcomes as the goal. To the degree that we can associate training and education with performance—that is, with results—we stand a better chance of delivering what is needed, when it is needed. We also reframe the whole activitity in terms of the employees, as they experience the delivery of skills and knowledge that are absolutely relevant to their needs and not simply a part of someone's "program." Finally, performance-based training is most likely to draw upon whatever resources meet the need.

To accomplish this, we might simply ask "Are we learning as much as we can?" or "Are we leveraging the knowledge, skills and capabilities of everyone in the organization?" If an organization or group is dedicated to learning, it builds incentives to share information, to teach others, and to seek help regardless of the position or role in the organization.

If an organization really wants to learn about its markets, its opportunities and about its own capacities, it will even accept failure as a learning experience.

All of these elements challenge and threaten traditional behaviors within organizations and within our educational systems. Because of this, the only way to get the change is to adopt an aggressive and enthusiastic commitment to creating the best possible opportunities for employees and students to learn. Our commitment will determine our ability to compete in the marketplace of the future.

PART 3

Managing Today for the Future

Creating a New Company Culture

Brian Dumaine

So it has come to this: You've automated the factory, decimated the inventory, eliminated the unnecessary from the organization chart, and the company still isn't hitting on all cylinders—and you've got an awful feeling you know why. It's the culture. It's the values, heroes, myths, symbols that have been in the organization forever, the attitudes that say, Don't disagree with the boss, or Don't make waves, or Just do enough to get by, or For God's sake, don't take chances. And how on earth are you going to change all *that*?

If your company is like a great many others, it will have to step up to this challenge. The changes businesses are being forced to make merely to stay competitive—improving quality, increasing speed, adopting a customer orientation—are so fundamental that they must take root in a company's very essence, which means in its culture. This news depresses those who remember corporate culture as the trendy concern of the mid-Eighties, when consultants ranging from the super-sober to the wacky tried to change companies' cultures and almost always found they couldn't. But take heart. An increasing number of enterprises are at last figuring out how to alter their cultures, and more than ever are doing it.

The basic lesson sounds like a Confucian principle: Cultural change must come from the bottom, and the CEO must guide it. Despite the apparent contradiction, Du Pont, Tandem Computers, and many others are making that idea work. Says Du Pont CEO Edgar Woolard: "Employees have been underestimated. You have to start with the premise that people at all levels want to contribute and make the business a success."

The CEO must show the direction of the change to make sure it happens coherently. But a cultural transformation is a change in the hearts and minds of the workers, and it won't happen if the CEO just talks. David Nadler, the president of Delta Consulting Group, warns of the plexiglass CEO syndrome: "CEOs encase their mission statement in plexiglass, hand it out, and people laugh. You have to change the way the person who assembles the machine or designs the product acts." This means the CEO must live the new culture, become the walking embodiment of it. He must also spot and celebrate managers and employees who exemplify the values he wants to inculcate.

No cultural change happens easily or quickly. Figure five to ten years for a significant improvement—but since the alternative may be extinction, it's worth a try. Here's how the most successful companies are changing their cultures today.

Beyond vision

Yes, a CEO must promulgate a vision, but the most brilliant vision statement this side of Paraguay won't budge a culture unless it's backed up by action. At a major manufacturer, a manager who preached quality found that a part in the tractors coming off his assembly line was defective and would burn out after 300 hours of use rather than the specified 1,000 hours—a problem the customer wouldn't notice for quite a while. The manager could ship the tractors and make his quarterly numbers, or he could fix the flaw. He decided to fix the flaw. His people now know he's serious about quality.

Du Pont CEO Woolard, who preaches that "nothing is worthwhile unless it touches the customer," understands that communicating isn't enough. At a number of his plants he has a program called Adopt a Customer, which encourages blue-collar workers to visit a customer once a month, learn his needs, and be his representative on the factory floor. As quality or delivery problems arise, the worker is more likely to see them from the customer's point of view and help make a decision that will keep his "adopted child" happy.

Management at Florida Power & Light is changing its culture from that of a bureaucratic backwater to one that worships quality and service. The company shows it is serious by giving even the lowliest employees extraordinary freedom to practice that religion. Example: The utility discovered that its meter readers suffered more on-the-job injuries than any other type of employee, and they were nasty ones—dog bites. The meter readers in Boca Raton wanted to form a team to study the problem. Under the old culture, management would have scoffed at such a notion as a waste of time. Says executive vice president Wayne Brunetti: "It would have been so easy for us to reject this kind of idea." But the new ethos allowed the meter readers to take the initiative. They formed a team of ten who surveyed households, found out which ones had fierce Fidos, and then programmed hand-held computers to beep just before a visit to a dangerous address. Dog bites (and absenteeism) are down, and morale (and service) is up.

Alter history

A company with the wrong history and myths can get itself in big trouble. For years after Walt Disney's death his ghost stalked the halls of the company's studios in Burbank, California, causing executives to freeze in their tracks and wonder, "What would Walt have done?"

These hero worshipers were driving the studio into the ground with an outdated line of family flicks. Realizing that sometimes history can't be changed without changing the players, CEO Michael Eisner came aboard and cleared the deck, bringing in new managers, most of whom had never met Disney. The new crew, freed of the spectral overseer, began to create a culture that was more sophisticated than stodgy, more adventurous than cautious, more ambitious than content. They have turned the company around by (among other moves) daring to make grownup films like *The Color of Money* and *Ruthless People*, which would have irked old Walt.

Can something as amorphous as history be changed without spilling blood? Consider what a Fortune 500 manufacturer did with a factory that had a history of poor quality, hostile labor relations, and terrible productivity. The company hired a consultant who started out by talking with the employees. They eagerly told him about Sam, the plant manager who was a 300-pound gorilla with a disposition that made King Kong look like Bonzo the chimp.

One time Sam examined a transmission, didn't like the work he saw, picked up a sledgehammer, and smashed it to pieces. A worker summoned to Sam's office threw up on the way. Another time Sam drove his car into the plant, got up on the roof, and started screaming at his workers. One worker, fed up, poured a line of gasoline to the car and lit it.

The stunned consultant made an appointment to see the plant manager. When he walked into the office he saw a slim, pleasant-looking man behind the desk; his name was Paul. "Where's Sam?" asked the consultant. Paul, looking puzzled, replied, "Sam has been dead for nine years."

From then on Paul and the consultant realized they had a serious problem. For years Paul had been trying to instill a sense of fairness and participation, but the plant's nightmarish history was so strong his efforts had failed. To cope, Paul and his supervisors sat down with groups of eight or ten assembly workers to discuss the plant's *history*—300-pound Sam and all. Just discussing it helped clear the air.

Paul also tried hard not to do anything Sam would have done. Once, while on the noisy shop floor, he abruptly pointed at a worker, commanding him to throw away a coffee cup left near a machine. Paul merely thought he was taking care of a safety hazard. The workers on the floor, mindful of the hateful Sam, thought something like, "Ah, he's just another militaristic S.O.B. who loves spit and polish." Better for Paul to have tossed the cup away himself—a small gesture, yet that and a thousand other subtle messages will eventually help transform a culture. After four years of effort, Paul's plant won his company's top award for quality.

Symbols, symbols, symbols

Paul learned, executives often underestimate the power symbolic gestures have on workers. Taking the corporate jet to a Hawaiian retreat to discuss cost cutting isn't exactly going to send the right message to the troops.

At Tandem, the computer company in Cupertino, California, a general manager once told CEO Jimmy Treybig that he wanted to fire an employee. Treybig said OK, but first find out why the person wasn't performing. The general manager discovered the employee had serious family problems and decided to give him another chance, sending a signal to everyone else in the company that we treat people around here with consideration. Says Treybig: "You have to keep remembering what your company is. All your work is done by your people."

Something as simple as an award can help make a culture more innovative. In Japan, Sharp rewards top performers by putting them on a "gold badge" project team that reports directly to the company president. The privilege instills pride and gets other employees scrambling for new ideas and products in the hope that they too may make the team.

Awards can also encourage risk taking. About a year ago, the people in Du Pont's relocation department—who help move executives to new cities—thought they could boost productivity by installing a new computer system. The experiment failed, but rather than chastise those who suggested it, the company in November presented them with a plaque that told them: We're proud of your effort and hope you try again as hard in years to come.

Create universities

Michael Beer, a Harvard business school professor, urges CEOs to identify models within the corporation. Scour the company to find some maverick manager who has figured out how to do it right—achieving high quality, good morale, innovative products. Then hold up this department or factory as a kind of university where employees can learn how others have succeeded. It's important not to force managers to adopt everything the university offers. Let them choose what works best for them.

In a study of six Fortune 500 companies that wanted to change their cultures, Beer found the only one that truly succeeded used the model approach. "With this one," says Beer, "the change began way before the CEO became fully aware of it. It was started in a small plant by some innovative managers. The top learned about it from the lowest level and spread the best practices around the company."

A caveat: The model concept works only when top management believes that *all* its employees have the ability to learn and grow. Too often a company stereotypes its blue-collar workers as dumb, inarticulate and mindlessly loyal to archaic values like macho exhibitionism and anti-intellectualism. Shake it, says Du Pont group vice president Mark Suwyn: "These people manage their lives well outside the factory. They sit on school boards or coach Little League. We have to create a culture where we can bring that creative energy into the work force."

Du Pont considers its plant in Towanda, Pennsylvania, which makes materials for printed circuitboards and other products, a model of the kind Beer is talking about. The plant, organized in self-directed work teams, lets employees find their own solutions to problems, set their own schedules, and even have a say in hiring. Managers call themselves facilitators, not bosses. Their main job is to coach workers and help them understand the tough, external market forces that demand a dedication to quality, teamwork, and speed. Over the past four years productivity at Towanda is up 35%.

Last spring Du Pont surveyed 6,600 of its people, including some at Towanda, and found that flexible work hours were a top priority. Working mothers and single parents said it was hard to cope with the kids while keeping to a rigid plant schedule. A team at Towanda got together and devised a novel solution: Take vacation time by the hour. During slack times when three of the four team members could easily handle the job, one could take off a few hours in the afternoon to go to a school play or bring a sick kid to the doctor. Today other Du Pont workers and managers visit Towanda to learn about flextime. A few have already borrowed it for their own plants.

Getting the most out of the university idea. CEO Woolard has found it helps to assign different goals of excellence to various Du Pont factories. He may tell the manager of one plant to be the best in team building, another the best in employee benefits, and a third the safety leader. As they improve, he holds up their accomplishments as examples to others. Says he: "It's win-win. You don't have to say one plant is a dog."

Trust starts from within

After a decade of restructuring, layoffs, and astronomical CEO salaries, worker trust has taken it on the chin. One of the biggest cultural challenges is to persuade workers to get religion again. It won't be easy. Making an angry, distrustful worker a believer requires fiddling with deep-rooted values. As almost any psychiatrist will tell you, it's a Herculean task to change a single individual. So imagine what it takes to change the beliefs of thousands.

Stephen Covey, a consultant to IBM, Hewlett-Packard, and other major companies, and author of *The 7 Habits of Highly Effective People,* believes every individual from the CEO down must realize that trust starts from within himself. Says he: "It's ludicrous to think that you can build trust unless people view you as trustworthy." In his seminars Covey gets managers to examine their deepest motives and to realize the importance of integrity and openness. And it's not all touchy-feely. Says Covey: "The best way our clients save money is to increase the span of control. When people trust you, you don't have to ride them, and that means fewer managers can oversee more people."

A manager can destroy a lot of trust by acting as if he's better than the people who work for him. Tandem CEO Treybig remembers suggesting that a couple of visiting managers spend a half day on the assembly line. They balked, thinking it a waste of time to mingle with blue-collar workers. "It was like you offered them syphilis," Treybig says.

He thought the idea made sense because much of Tandem's long-term success, he believes, comes from treating people as equals. For the past 15 years Tandem every Friday afternoon has put on its legendary get-togethers, once known as beer busts but now called popcorn parties (the Tandemites don't drink like they used to). Here Treybig and his top managers mix with the troops and exchange ideas about what's bad, what's good, and what can be done better in the company. As a bonus, employees from different parts of the business share ideas about the latest technologies. Four times a year Treybig spends five days in different resorts around the country with a couple of hundred people from all levels of the corporation. They talk business, play, drink beer until 2 A.M. and generally learn to trust each other. Says Treybig: "They'll go back and tell fellow employees that you care about people."

Du Pont CEO Woolard argues that the best way to create a more trusting environment is to reward the right people. "The first thing people watch," says he, "is the kind of people you promote. Are you promoting team builders who spend time on relationships, or those who are autocratic?"

Covey agrees, adding that managers should tailor reward systems to recognize team effort rather than individual accomplish-

Keys to change

Understand your old culture first. You can't chart a course until you know where you are.

Encourage those employees who are bucking the old culture and have ideas for a better one.

Find the best subculture in your organization, and hold it up as an example from which others can learn.

Don't attack culture head on. Help employees find their own new ways to accomplish their tasks, and a better culture will follow.

Don't count on a vision to work miracles. At best it acts as a guiding principle for change.

Figure on five to ten years for significant, organization-wide improvement.

Live the culture you want. As always, action speaks louder than words.

ment. As the wrong way to do it, he cites a CEO who would call his managers into his office each week to talk about team spirit. At the end of the meeting he'd point to a large painting of racehorses with photos of the managers' faces pasted over the thoroughbreds' heads. Then he'd announce, "So and so is ahead in the race to win the trip to Bermuda." Says Covey: "It nullified everything he said earlier."

Trying to change an institution's culture is certain to be frustrating. Most people resist change, and when the changes goes to the basic character of the place where they earn a living, many people will get upset. Says the University of Pittsburgh's Kilmann: "If you talk about real change and people aren't getting uptight and anxious, they don't believe you." Some will fight. After months of working on cultural change with employees of a company, Kilmann asked the group to write down what they were doing differently. One manager wrote: "I wore a different color tie."

Managers seeking a way to think about the process might reflect that a company trying to improve its culture is like a person trying to improve his or her character. The process is long, difficult, often agonizing. The only reason people put themselves through it is that it's correspondingly satisfying and valuable.

No, You Don't Manage Everyone the Same

Jim Braham

"Let's talk about stereotypes," George Arteaga prodded. "What's the first thing that comes to mind when I say Anglo-Saxon?" The 20 Minneapolis district sales and service managers attending Wang Laboratories' one-day training course in "Managing a Diverse Workforce" hesitated briefly. Then the replies flew.

"White," one manager spoke up. "European," another said. "Middle class." "Blond, blue-eyed."

"All right," said the company's human-resources development consultant, "what's the first thing you think when I say Jewish? Italian? Greek? Again, we're talking stereotypes."

"Hot-tempered," one manager said. "Dark hair," said another. "Money." "Expressive."

"O. K., what about Asians?"

"Small." "Shifty." "Scientific." "They expect women to be submissive."

"How about blacks?"

"Pro basketball." "Inner city." "They expect things to be handed to them."

"What do you think of when I say Hispanic?" asked Mr. Arteaga, who was born in Mexico.

"Good lovers," one manager said. "Bluecollar." "Immigrant."

"What about American Indians?"

"Lazy," was one reply. "Drinking," another said.

In identifying and discussing stereotypes about races, national origins and cultures, and gender—as well as age and disability—and then showing how biases and assumptions aren't true and can cripple companies as well as individuals, Wang Laboratories and other progressive corporations are preparing their managers to deal with a very different workforce ahead, one composed more and more of minorities and women.

These corporate leaders—among them Mobil Corp., Apple Computer, Xerox, Digital Equipment, Procter & Gamble, Honeywell, and Hewlett-Packard—are approaching this in a daring, drastically different manner from the way business previously treated the issue. The old approach, spurred by equal-employment opportunity (EEO) directives, said: Everyone's basically the same; therefore manage everyone the same way. Some companies—primarily those requiring a less-skilled workforce—still follow that practice.

More corporate leaders, however, now realize: Everyone's *not* the same; there are differences among us, which become more evident the more minority employees a company has. These differences can and do sometimes present problems but they also can strengthen a company. We should *recognize* these differences and be aware of them. We should *value* this diversity and learn to manage in such a way that, as Apple Computer's Santiago Rodriguez states, "you don't manage everyone the *same*—you manage everyone *fairly*. There is a difference."

"No one manages everyone the same," says Apple's new manager of multicultural and affirmative-action programs. "People say they do, but if you watch them, they don't—because everyone knows that different individuals, even if they are all from the same background, are motivated by different stimuli."

In this new approach to a changing workforce, business is moving into difficult, sensitive areas. To even discuss differences and stereotypes is to risk reinforcing and perpetuating them.

"There's no question that it's easier to manage people who are the same, but we are not, and it is not our similarities that cause our problem. There are real racial, cultural, ethnic, and gender differences that we have to work on," says Lewis Griggs, an ex-consultant who's now president of Copeland Griggs Productions. His San Francisco firm produced a three-video training series called "Valuing Diversity" that's sponsored by 30 major corporations and is a key part of present company training.

In it, David Kearns, chairman and CEO of Xerox Corp., warns: "We have to manage diversity right now, and much more so in the future. American business will not be able to survive if we do not have a large, diverse workforce, because those are the demographics.

"If you fail to include women and minorities, you've restricted yourself from a major part of the labor pool, which economically doesn't make sense. But beyond that, one of the major advantages you get out of having women and minorities in business is that they bring a whole new set of ideas. And right now, American business needs new ideas and thoughts if we're going to compete on a world-wide basis.

"You can't just hire large numbers of women and minorities and think it'll work," Mr. Kearns cautions. "You need a process to identify the right experiences people will need to move ahead. You need to have training programs for your managers that talk about managing diversity. What are the issues of managing minorities and women, because there are things that are different."

No longer an EEO issue, valuing and managing a diverse workforce is chiefly an upward-mobility issue affecting the bottom line. One reason it's gaining so much attention is that affirmative action really hasn't worked. Women and minorities remain concentrated in the lower ranks.

Wang Laboratories already has put more than 1,000 managers—essentially white males—through its managing-diversity training. In the daylong session in Minneapolis the managers learned about the changing labor picture; discovered the folly of making assumptions about others; viewed and discussed a "Valuing Diversity" tape; addressed the role of a leader in a diverse workforce; were briefed on equal-opportunity laws and debated related management problems; were updated on sexual-harassment regulations and problems; discussed stereotypes; and watched "A Class Divided." This video illustrates the crushing impact of discrimination upon schoolchildren separated into superior and inferior groups by "blue eyes" and "brown eyes."

Wang's program is built upon four basic "building blocks," says Cle Jackson, the firm's director of human services for U. S. operations. "These are awareness of your behavior; acknowledgement of your biases and stereotypes; focus on job performance; and avoidance of assumptions."

All this is dictated by the bottom line, he says. "You've got to get maximum productivity out of employees. Discrimination, and not being able to manage a diverse workforce, will cost the company a lot of money. If you plan to work for this company, you're going to have to modify your behavior and understand how to deal with people unlike yourself.

"If you're a salesperson and you have hang-ups about dealing with people of color, if you have problems selling to a black, you're going to lose money for the corporation, and we don't need you.

"If a senior-level woman is responsible for buying your product and you have problems dealing with women, we don't need you. If you treat an employee wrong, disparagingly, or different, it's going to cost Wang a lot of money in lawsuits."

In diversity training the major obstacle companies must overcome is "getting managers to accept that they have a problem," Mr. Jackson says. "That's denial."

All this attention on valuing and managing diversity is sparked by the startling changes forecast for the American workforce between 1986 and 2000:

Only 32% of the workers entering the labor force will be white, non-Hispanic males, the U. S. Bureau of Labor Statistics forecasts. They already have declined to 44% of all employees, according to the last count in 1986.

Women will account for 51% of the growth.

Hispanics, the fastest-growing minority, will represent 15% of the entering workers.

Blacks will represent 13% of the entering workers.

Asians and other minorities will account for 6% of all new workers.

By 2000 the workforce will comprise (1986 estimates in parentheses): white, non-Hispanic males 39% (44%), women 47% (45%), blacks 12% (11%), Hispanics 10% (7%), Asians and others 4% (3%).

Note that the figures for women and minorities overlap, and Hispanics may be of any race, although it's estimated that 97% of those in the U. S. are white.

Some sections of the nation, of course, are more affected than others. For example, as Apple's Mr. Rodriguez points out, "In California in the next ten years there won't be a majority, so the whole idea of minority is irrelevant. White Americans will be the largest minority and around the year 2005 Hispanics will become the largest minority."

In one-day or even week-long managing-diversity training, companies don't hope to completely change lifetime attitudes, of course; the process must be ongoing. What this training does is at least make managers (and subordinates) *aware* of the issue.

"You can't manage diversity if you don't identify it as an issue," says Mr. Rodriguez. Born in Harlem of Puerto Rican descent, the former consultant has started managers discussing "why multiculturalism is essential for the company. The idea is that every culture has something to offer, from a value-added business perspective to how we manage our workforce."

As an example of cultural differences, he says, "It is rude in East Asian cultures to answer a question in the negative. People will tell you yes even when they mean no. So we need to train people not to ask binary questions that require a yes or no answer. There are other ways to get that information."

In Hispanic as well as Asian cultures, modesty is ingrained. "I was raised with the notion that if you're good, someone will know about it. You never talk about yourself," Mr. Rodriguez notes. So, to single out an Hispanic or Asian and praise him or her publicly "could be terribly embarrassing in my subculture, especially if my ethnic peers are in the group.

"There are different ways one can reward—privately, for example. This is what a manager has to be attuned to. But you have to be careful, because you also can be stereotypical. Obviously, many Hispanics are thoroughly Anglicized, so that's not an issue [for them]. This is a very tricky area."

Indeed. When this white male reporter originally described this article as "managing minorities," he discovered that the term offended minorities. "It is very condescending because it assumes only white males manage minorities," says King Ming Young, manager of the managing-diversity program at Hewlett-Packard Co. (H-P). "We're talking about women managing men, blacks managing white males, Asians managing Hispanics, and so forth.

"The whole emphasis of managing diversity is that it takes us away from the affirmative-action mindset that either the woman or the minority person is deficient in some ways. We need to recognize that every person is different and not necessarily better than the others, and that we're all in this together, including white males. We need to look at how, because of our cultural conditioning, we might have difficulties working together, and how to make the most of that situation, because we *are* different.

"We need to create an environment that permits diversity to grow," Ms. Young continues. "We need to dispel some myths and acknowledge cultural differences—which sometimes is a paradox, it's a matter of degree—and not be judgmental about those differences."

"You have to first defuse stereotypical attitudes," says Chet Garron, training manager for the valuing-differences and valuing-diversity programs at Digital Equipment. "What gets people in trouble are such concepts as 'all blacks are lazy and like to dance,' 'all Hispanics will cut your throat and are wetbacks,' 'all Asians are brilliant and don't like to talk about themselves,' 'all women overreact and are emotional,' and so forth."

Asked for a white male stereotype, Mr. Garron, who is black, suggests: "White males discount or invalidate everybody. The only thing white males are comfortable doing is working with other white males."

Wang Laboratories' Mr. Jackson, also black, observes that blacks and Hispanics approach situations more in a "man-to-man" or "feeling, caring" manner, while white men function primarily in a "man-to-object" style based upon power. To a black, "feeling" is all-important and if a white manager comes off "non-caring," he says, "the black is going to construe it as racism, even when it's not. Then you have rebellion."

"The most successful white managers are very much in touch with their feelings," he points out. "Most discrimination takes place at middle management, because of the low comfort level there."

Apple Computer's Mr. Rodriquez suggests a practice that works in the Hispanic culture: "If you come to my office to visit, chances are we will spend five to ten minutes talking about non-business issues—unless there's an emergency."

One roadblock, involving blacks in particular, is our "racial taboo," he observes. "Unself-conscious discussions about race in racially mixed settings do not occur in America today. People don't feel comfortable even discussing this subject. But you can't manage diversity if you don't identify it as an issue. This is the No. 1 task for corporate America."

A "presumption of incompetence is another issue of which managers should be aware, Mr. Rodriguez says. "White males [typically] are presumed to be competent unless proved otherwise. Minorities and women are presumed to be incompetent until proven otherwise."

A feeling of always being tested also affects minorities and women. "We all make mistakes," says Mr. Rodriguez, "but when white men make them it's not assumed [it's] because they're white. It's often presumed about women and minorities that they make mistakes because they *are* women and minorities."

Apple Computer's managerial training also will explore "what it means to be a minority in a majority society," Mr. Rodriguez says. Example: "Majorities don't pay much attention to minorities not being present. But minorities always notice. As an Hispanic, wherever I go I notice whether people of color are there or not. This is not a black-white issue, it's a majority issue."

Thus, he says, "if you're selling to someone with a large minority representation, it's likely they'll notice what your sales staff looks like. If it doesn't look the way they think it should, it could have an impact on your business. This is a value added in terms of diversity, so that you not only sell better but also know better what products people need."

At H-P, managing diversity is the next logical step from its commitment to affirmative action, says Ms. Young. While the company has about 45% women and nearly 20% minority employees, minorities fill perhaps 2% of upper-management positions, as they do at many large corporations, she observes.

"To probe, we have to look at the cultural environment. What are some of the ways that people may be barred from climbing the organizational hierarchy? The manager-subordinate relationship is the key focus. What do managers need to do to provide equality of opportunities for people who are very different from themselves?" asks the former consultant, who was born in Hong Kong, raised in Honduras, and educated in America.

Communications and culture are major considerations. "There is greater probability of misunderstanding when people of different backgrounds work together," Ms. Young says. "And there is greater probability that when people promote others and seek others to join their teams, they unconsciously seek people who are similar to themselves and with whom they feel comfortable. That's human nature. But by choosing certain people, we exclude others who may be equally or more qualified."

The first step in the H-P approach is to make managers aware of the biases and assumptions that control their "comfort zones and boundaries," and then show how these harm people and the company.

Example: A manager feels he cannot honestly assess a woman's performance because "she's not strong enough, she won't stand up for her beliefs." Yet, if he tells her the truth, "she will think I'm a chauvinist." Result: "Both parties lose," Ms. Young says. "The woman (or minority) fails to get feedback that can lead her to success, and the company loses because it might have missed the opportunity to develop someone with great potential."

Foreign accents also can create discomfort, by "irritating native speakers of English" and thus distracting attention from speech content. The H-P manager calls for "a greater tolerance for difference, a recognition that sometimes without knowing it people judge others based on appearance or accents." For example, she notes that French, British, and German accents are evaluated positively—"we think French is chic"—while a Vietnamese or Cantonese accent causes negative response.

In asking us to "take the time to understand" those with accents, she declares that minorities "also need to make conscious efforts to improve their speaking ability. It's not all a one-way street."

The cultural differences of which managers should be aware frequently concern the "boss-subordinate relationship," Ms. Young observes. Asians grow up with a "greater acceptance of authority and it's perfectly acceptable for a manager to tell subordinates exactly what to do. If a subordinate questions this, it's not appropriate." At the other extreme, she points to Scandinavian countries where the "subordinate and manager have almost equal power, the subordinate questions decisions, and gets a bigger role in decisionmaking." The U. S. ranks "in the middle" of this "power/ distance" relationship, she says.

"Respect for authority, modesty, and harmony are three values Asians hold very dear," she continues. "If a manager is aware that it would be very difficult for someone from a cultural system that values humility and modesty to verbalize his own accomplishments, the manager might ask specifically: 'What was your role in this project?'"

Coming from a culture that calls for silence "unless you have something profound to say," Ms. Young herself had to battle cultural obstacles during her American consulting career. "People were always looking to my male counterpart for final say when I was really in charge," she relates. "When I did not brag about myself, people thought I didn't do anything and had few accomplishments. I learned you have to be able to recount your accomplishments without being obnoxious. It used to be very difficult when people asked what I had done. Now I feel a little more comfortable."

It also used to be much more difficult for her to socialize, Ms. Young admits. "People in companies do not realize how much business gets done through small, informal talk. If you can't tell jokes, if you don't respond appropriately to punch lines, people dismiss you. People in power are always kidding with each other and if you cannot participate in that kind of social conversation, you are really left out, no matter how smart you are."

Ms. Young spent two years developing, testing, and then preparing approximately 100 trainers to present H-P's managing-diversity program to managers around the world. In December, that program, covering one to three days, was put in operation.

For two years, Mobil Corp. also has been conducting managing-and valuing-diversity programs. It runs a three-day program for supervisors and managers, and more than 150 people have attended, 20 at a time. "The issues are not overt discrimination—but subtleties," says Robert Kleeb Jr., manager of labor relations and EEO. Supervisors are confronted with scenarios such as this:

"Do you have an assumption that blacks are less qualified than whites, and therefore you should expect less from them, and therefore you don't hold them to the same standard that you would a white, and therefore you don't counsel and encourage and reprimand and everything else you would do with a white person to improve his performance? And therefore," Mr. Kleeb concludes, "as a result of not having that coaching and counseling, blacks *don't* get as far."

Mobil also operates two three-day programs for minority employees "to air some of their concerns and the impediments they see and to determine whether *they* are contributing in any way to limiting their own development," he adds.

Not all companies embrace this concept of valuing and managing a diverse workforce, of course. "We buried these issues years ago and there's no way we're raising them again," one company told Copeland Griggs' Mr. Griggs.

"They seem to think that by making everyone treat everyone the same—and some people even use those words—they avoid the problems," the film producer adds. "I ask them if they've asked their nonwhite males [and women] how *they* feel about being treated the same, and whether *they* think there are no problems. They say no, we don't need to—it's nice and peaceful here."

Regarded by large corporations as basically an issue of upward mobility, managing diversity so far affects white collar more than blue collar ranks. "There's greater human potential there to be tapped," H-P's Ms. Young observes. "And the concept that we treat people fairly, but not equally, doesn't work in a union environment— because there you want to treat people exactly the same. You don't want to recognize their differences."

This whole idea of fair treatment goes above and beyond even the golden rule. Today the experts say: No longer should we treat people as we would like them to treat us, which we were raised to do. Now we should treat people *as they would like us to treat them.*

The New Managerial Work

Rosabeth Moss Kanter

Managerial work is undergoing such enormous and rapid change that many managers are reinventing their profession as they go. With little precedent to guide them, they are watching hierarchy fade away and the clear distinctions of title, task, department, even corporation, blur. Faced with extraordinary levels of complexity and interdependency, they watch traditional sources of power erode and the old motivational tools lose their magic.

The cause is obvious. Competitive pressures are forcing corporations to adopt new flexible strategies and structures. Many of these are familiar: acquisitions and divestitures aimed at more focused combinations of business activities, reductions in management staff and levels of hierarchy, increased use of performance-based rewards. Other strategies are less common but have an even more profound effect. In a growing number of companies, for example, horizontal ties between peers are replacing vertical ties as channels of activity and communication. Companies are asking corporate staffs and functional departments to play a more strategic role with greater cross-departmental collaboration. Some organizations are turning themselves nearly inside out—buying formerly internal services from outside suppliers, forming strategic alliances and supplier-customer partnerships that bring external relationships inside where they can influence company policy and practice. I call these emerging practices "postentrepreneurial" because they involve the application of entrepreneurial creativity and flexibility to established businesses.

Such changes come highly recommended by the experts who urge organizations to become leaner, less bureaucratic, more entrepreneurial. But so far, theorists have given scant attention to the dramatically altered realities of managerial work in these transformed corporations. We don't even have good words to describe the new relationships. "Superiors" and "subordinates" hardly seem accurate, and even "bosses" and "their people" imply more control and ownership than managers today actually possess. On top of it all, career paths are no longer straightforward and predictable but have become idiosyncratic and confusing.

Some managers experience the new managerial work as a loss of power because much of their authority used to come from hierarchical position. Now that everything seems negotiable by everyone, they are confused about how to mobilize and motivate staff. For other managers, the shift in roles and tasks offers greater personal power. The following case histories illustrate the responses of three managers in three different industries to the opportunities and dilemmas of structural change.

Hank is vice president and chief engineer for a leading heavy equipment manufacturer that is moving aggressively against foreign competition. One of the company's top priorities has been to increase the speed, quality, and cost-effectiveness of product development. So Hank worked with consultants to improve collaboration between manufacturing and other functions and to create closer alliances between the company and its outside suppliers. Gradually, a highly segmented operation became an integrated process involving project teams drawn from component divisions, functional departments, and external suppliers. But along the way, there were several unusual side effects. Different areas of responsibility overlapped. Some technical and manufacturing people were co-located. Liaisons from functional areas joined the larger development teams. Most unusual of all, project teams had a lot of direct contact with higher levels of the company.

Many of the managers reporting to Hank felt these changes as a loss of power. They didn't always know what their people were doing, but they still believed they ought to know. They no longer had sole input into performance appraisals; other people from other functions had a voice as well, and some of them knew more about employees' project performance. New career paths made it less important to please direct superiors in order to move up the functional line.

Moreover, employees often bypassed Hank's managers and interacted directly with decision makers inside and outside the company. Some of these so-called subordinates had contact with division executives and senior corporate staff, and sometimes they sat in on high-level strategy meetings to which their managers were not invited.

At first Hank thought his managers' resistance to the new process was just the normal noise associated with any change. Then he began to realize that something more profound was going on. The reorganization was challenging traditional notions about the role and power of managers and shaking traditional hierarchy to its roots. And no one could see what was taking its place.

When George became head of a major corporate department in a large bank holding company, he thought he had arrived. His title and rank were unmistakable, and his department was responsible for determining product-line policy for hundreds of bank branches and the virtual clerks—in George's eyes—who managed them. George staffed his department with MBAs and promised them rapid promotion.

Then the sand seemed to shift beneath him. Losing market position for the first time in recent memory, the bank decided to emphasize direct customer service at the branches. The people George considered clerks began to depart from George's standard policies and to tailor their services to local market conditions. In many cases, they actually demanded services and responses from George's staff, and the results of their requests began to figure in performance reviews of George's department. George's people were spending more and more time in the field with branch managers, and the corporate personnel department was even trying to assign some of George's MBAs to branch and regional posts.

To complicate matters, the bank's strategy included a growing role for technology. George felt that because he had no direct control over the information systems department, he should not be held fully accountable for every facet of product design and implementation. But fully accountable he was. He had to deploy people to learn the new technology and figure out how to work with it. Furthermore, the bank was asking product departments like George's to find ways to link existing products or develop new ones that crossed traditional categories. So George's people were often away on cross-departmental teams just when he wanted them for some internal assignment.

Instead of presiding over a tidy empire the way his predecessor had, George presided over what looked to him like chaos. The bank said senior executives should be "leaders, not managers," but George didn't know what that meant, especially since he seemed to have lost control over his subordinates' assignments, activities, rewards, and careers. He resented his perceived loss of status.

The CEO tried to show him that good results achieved the new way would bring great monetary rewards, thanks to a performance-based bonus program that was gradually replacing more modest yearly raises. But the pressures on George were also greater, unlike anything he'd ever experienced.

For Sally, purchasing manager at an innovative computer company, a new organizational strategy was a gain rather than a loss, although it changed her relationship with the people reporting to her. Less than ten years out of college, she was hired as an analyst—a semiprofessional, semiclerical job—then promoted to a purchasing manager's job in a sleepy staff department. She didn't expect to go much further in what was then a well-established hierarchy. But after a shocking downturn, top management encouraged employees to rethink traditional ways of doing things. Sally's boss, the head of purchasing, suggested that "partnerships" with key suppliers might improve quality, speed innovation, and reduce costs.

Soon Sally's backwater was at the center of policymaking, and Sally began to help shape strategy. She organized meetings between her company's senior executives and supplier CEOs. She sent her staff to contribute supplier intelligence at company seminars on technical innovation, and she spent more of her own time with product designers and manufacturing planners. She led senior executives on a tour of supplier facilities, traveling with them in the corporate jet.

Because some suppliers were also important customers, Sally's staff began meeting frequently with marketing managers to share information and address joint problems. Sally and her group were now also acting as internal advocates for major suppliers. Furthermore, many of these external companies now contributed performance appraisals of Sally and her team, and their opinions weighed almost as heavily as those of her superiors.

As a result of the company's new direction, Sally felt more personal power and influence, and her ties to peers in other areas and to top management were stronger. But she no longer felt like a manager directing subordinates. Her staff had become a pool of resources deployed by many others besides Sally. She was exhilarated by her personal opportunities but not quite sure the people she managed should have the same freedom to choose their own assignments. After all, wasn't that a manager's prerogative?

Hank's, George's and Sally's very different stories say much about the changing nature of managerial work. However hard it is for managers at the very top to remake strategy and structure, they themselves will probably retain their identity, status, and control. For the managers below them, structural change is often much harder. As work units become more participative and team oriented, and as professionals and knowledge workers become more prominent, the distinction between manager and nonmanager begins to erode.

To understand what managers must do to achieve results in the postentrepreneurial corporation, we need to look at the changing picture of how such companies operate. The picture has five elements:

1. There are a greater number and variety of channels for taking action and exerting influence.
2. Relationships of influence are shifting from the vertical to the horizontal, from chain of command to peer networks.
3. The distinction between managers and those managed is diminishing, especially in terms of information, control over assignments, and access to external relationships.
4. External relationships are increasingly important as sources of internal power and influence, even of career development.
5. As a result of the first four changes, career development has become less intelligible but also less circumscribed. There are fewer assured routes to success, which produces anxiety. At the same time, career paths are more open to innovation, which produces opportunity.

To help companies implement their competitive organizational strategies, managers must learn new ways to manage, confronting changes in their own bases of power and recognizing the need for new ways to motivate people.

The bases of power

The changes I've talked about can be scary for people like George and the managers reporting to Hank, who were trained to know their place, to follow orders, to let the company take care of their careers, to do things by the book. The book is gone. In the new corporation, managers have only themselves to count on for success. They must learn to operate without the crutch of hierarchy. Position, title, and authority are no longer adequate tools, not in a world where subordinates are encouraged to think for themselves and where managers have to work synergistically with other departments and even other companies. Success depends increasingly on tapping into sources of good ideas, on figuring out whose collaboration is needed to act on those ideas, on working with both to produce results. In short, the new managerial work implies very different ways of obtaining and using power.

The postentrepreneurial corporation is not only leaner and flatter, it also has many more channels for action. Cross-functional projects, business-unit joint ventures, labor-management forums, innovation funds that spawn activities outside mainstream budgets and reporting lines, strategic partnerships with suppliers or customers—these are all overlays on the traditional organization chart, strategic pathways that ignore the chain of command.

Their existence has several important implications. For one thing, they create more potential centers of power. As the ways to combine resources increase, the ability to command diminishes. Alternative paths of communication, resource access, and execution erode the authority of those in the nominal chain of command. In other words, the opportunity for greater speed and flexibility undermines hierarchy. As more and more strategic action takes place in these channels, the jobs that focus inward on particular departments decline in power.

As a result, the ability of managers to get things done depends more on the number of networks in which they're centrally involved than on their height in a hierarchy. Of course, power in any organization always has a network component, but rank and formal structure used to be more limiting. For example, access to information and the ability to get informal backing were often confined to the few officially sanctioned contact points between departments or between the company and its vendors or customers. Today these official barriers are disappearing, while so-called informal networks grow in importance.

In the emerging organization, managers add value by deal making, by brokering at interfaces, rather than by presiding over their individual empires. It was traditionally the job of top executives or specialists to scan the business environment for new ideas, opportunities, and resources. This kind of environmental scanning is now an important part of a manager's job at every level and in every function. And the environment to be scanned includes various company divisions, many potential outside partners, and large parts of the world. At the same time, people are encouraged to think about what they know that might have value elsewhere. An engineer designing windshield wipers, for example, might discover properties of rubber adhesion to glass that could be useful in other manufacturing areas.

Every manager must think cross-functionally because every department has to play a strategic role, understanding and contributing to other facets of the business. In Hank's company, the technical managers and staff working on design engineering used to concentrate only on their own areas of expertise. Under the new system, they have to keep in mind what manufacturing does and how it does it. They need to visit plants and build relationships so they can ask informed questions.

One multinational corporation, eager to extend the uses of its core product, put its R&D staff and laboratory personnel in direct contact with marketing experts to discuss lines of research. Similarly, the superior economic track record of Raytheon's New Products Center—dozens of new products and patents yielding profits many times their development costs—derives from the connections it builds between its inventors and the engineering and marketing staffs of the business units it serves.

This strategic and collaborative role is particularly important for the managers and professionals on corporate staffs. They need to serve as integrators and facilitators, not as watchdogs and interventionists. They need to sell their services, justify themselves to the business units they serve, literally compete with outside suppliers. General Foods recently put overhead charges for corporate staff services on a pay-as-you-use basis. Formerly, these charges were either assigned uniformly to users and nonusers alike, or the services were mandatory. Product managers sometimes had to work through as many as eight layers of management and corporate staff to get business plans approved. Now these staffs must prove to the satisfaction of their internal customers that their services add value.

By contrast, some banks still have corporate training departments that do very little except get in the way. They do no actual training, for example, yet they still exercise veto power over urgent divisional training decisions and consultant contracts.

As managers and professionals spend more time working across boundaries with peers and partners over whom they have no direct control, their negotiating skills become essential assets. Alliances and partnerships transform impersonal, arm's-length contracts into relationships involving joint planning and joint decision making. Internal competitors and adversaries become allies on whom managers depend for their own success. At the same time, more managers at more levels are active in the kind of external diplomacy that only the CEO or selected staffs used to conduct.

In the collaborative forums that result, managers are more personally exposed. It is trust that makes partnerships work. Since collaborative ventures often bring together groups with different methods, cultures, symbols, even languages, good deal making depends on empathy—the ability to step into other people's shoes and appreciate their goals. This applies not only to intricate global joint ventures but also to the efforts of engineering and manufacturing to work together more effectively. Effective communication in a cooperative effort rests on more than a simple exchange of information; people must be adept at anticipating the responses of other groups. "Before I get too excited about our department's design ideas," an engineering manager told me, "I'm learning to ask myself, 'What's the marketing position on this? What will manufacturing say?' That sometimes forces me to make changes before I even talk to them."

An increase in the number of channels for strategic contact within the postentrepreneurial organization means more opportunities for people with ideas or information to trigger action: salespeople encouraging account managers to build strategic partnerships with customers, for example, or technicians searching for ways to tap new-venture funds to develop software. Moreover, top executives who have to spend more time on cross-boundary relationships are forced to delegate more responsibility to lower level managers. Delegation is one more blow to hierarchy, of course, since subordinates with greater responsibility are bolder about speaking up, challenging authority, and charting their own course.

For example, it is common for new-venture teams to complain publicly about corporate support departments and to reject their use in favor of external service providers, often to the consternation of more orthodox superiors. A more startling example occurred in a health care company where members of a task force charged with finding synergies among three lines of business shocked corporate executives by criticizing upper management behavior in their report. Service on the task force had created collective awareness of a shared problem and had given people the courage to confront it.

The search for internal synergies, the development of strategic alliances, and the push for new ventures all emphasize the political side of a leader's work. Executives must be able to juggle a set of constituencies rather than control a set of subordinates. They have to bargain, negotiate, and sell instead of making unilateral decisions and issuing commands. The leader's task, as Chester Barnard recognized long ago, is to develop a network of cooperative relationships among all the people, groups, and organizations that have something to contribute to an economic enterprise. Postentrepreneurial strategies magnify the complexity of this task. After leading Teknowledge, a producer of expert systems software, through development alliances with six corporations including General Motors and Procter & Gamble, company chairman Lee Hecht said he felt like the mayor of a small city. "I have a constituency that won't quit. It takes a hell of a lot of balancing." The kind of power achieved through a network of stakeholders is very different from the kind of power managers wield in a traditional bureaucracy. The new way gets more done, but it also takes more time. And it creates an illusion about freedom and security.

The absence of day-to-day constraints, the admonition to assume responsibility, the pretense of equality, the elimination of visible status markers, the prevalence of candid dialogues across hierarchical levels—these can give employees a false sense that all hierarchy is a thing of the past. Yet at the same time, employees still count on hierarchy to shield them when things go wrong. This combination would create the perfect marriage of freedom and support—freedom when people want to take risks, support when the risks don't work out.

In reality, less benevolent combinations are also possible, combinations not of freedom and support but of insecurity and loss of control. There is often a pretense in postentrepreneurial companies that status differences have nothing to do with power, that the deference paid to top executives derives from their superior qualifications rather than from the power they have over the fates of others.

But the people at the top of the organization chart still wield power —and sometimes in ways that managers below them experience as arbitrary. Unprecedented individual freedom also applies to top managers, who are now free to make previously unimaginable deals, order unimaginable cuts, or launch unimaginable takeovers. The re-organizations that companies undertake in their search for new synergies can uncover the potential unpredictability and capricious-ness of corporate careers. A man whose company was undergoing drastic restructuring told me, "For all of my ownership share and strategic centrality and voice in decisions, I can still be faced with a shift in direction not of my own making. I can still be reorganized into a corner. I can still be relocated into oblivion. I can still be re-viewed out of my special project budget."

These realities of power, change, and job security are important because they affect the way people view their leaders. When the illu-sion of simultaneous freedom and protection fades, the result can be a loss of motivation.

Sources of motivation

One of the essential, unchanging tasks of leaders is to motivate and guide performance. But motivational tools are changing fast. More and more businesses are doing away with the old bureaucratic in-centives and using entrepreneurial opportunity to attract the best talent. Managers must exercise more leadership even as they watch their bureaucratic power slip away. Leadership, in short, is more difficult yet more critical than ever.

Because of the unpredictability of even the most benign re-structuring, managers are less able to guarantee a particular job— or any job at all—no matter what a subordinate's performance level. The reduction in hierarchical levels curtails a manager's abil-ity to promise promotion. New compensation systems that make bo-nuses and raises dependent on objective performance measures and on team appraisals deprive managers of their role as the sole arbi-ters of higher pay. Cross-functional and cross-company teams can rob managers of their right to direct or even understand the work their so-called subordinates do. In any case, the shift from routine work, which was amenable to oversight, to "knowledge" work, which often is not, erodes a manager's claim to superior expertise. And partnerships and ventures that put lower level people in direct contact with each other across departmental and company bound-aries cut heavily into the managerial monopoly on information. At a consumer packaged-goods manufacturer that replaced several lev-els of hierarchy with teams, plant team members in direct contact with the sales force often had data on product ordering trends be-fore the higher level brand managers who set product policy.

As if the loss of carrots and sticks was not enough, many managers can no longer even give their people clear job standards and easily mastered procedural rules. Postentrepreneurial corporations seek problem-solving, initiative-taking employees who will go the unexpected extra mile for the customer. To complicate the situation further still, the complexities of work in the new organization—projects and relationships clamoring for attention in every direction—exacerbate the feeling of overload.

With the old motivational tool kit depleted, leaders need new and more effective incentives to encourage high performance and build commitment. There are five new tools:

Mission Helping people believe in the importance of their work is essential, especially when other forms of certainty and security have disappeared. Good leaders can inspire others with the power and excitement of their vision and give people a sense of purpose and pride in their work. Pride is often a better source of motivation than the traditional corporate career ladder and the promotion-based reward system. Technical professionals, for example, are often motivated most effectively by the desire to see their work contribute to an excellent final product.

Agenda control As career paths lose their certainty and companies' futures grow less predictable, people can at least be in charge of their own professional lives. More and more professionals are passing up jobs with glamour and prestige in favor of jobs that give them greater control over their own activities and direction. Leaders give their subordinates this opportunity when they give them release time to work on pet projects, when they emphasize results instead of procedures, and when they delegate work and the decisions about how to do it. Choice of their next project is a potent reward for people who perform well.

Share of value creation Entrepreneurial incentives that give teams a piece of the action are highly appropriate in collaborative companies. Because extra rewards are based only on measurable results, this approach also conserves resources. Innovative companies are experimenting with incentives like phantom stock for development of new ventures and other strategic achievements, equity participation in project returns, and bonuses pegged to key performance targets. Given the cross-functional nature of many projects today, rewards of this kind must sometimes be systemwide, but individual managers can also ask for a bonus pool for their own areas, contingent, of course, on meeting performance goals. And everyone can share the kinds of rewards that are abundant and free—awards and recognition.

Learning The chance to learn new skills or apply them in new arenas is an important motivator in a turbulent environment because it's oriented toward securing the future. "The learning organization" promises to become a 1990s business buzzword as companies seek to learn more systematically from their experience and to encourage continuous learning for their people. In the world of high technology, where people understand uncertainty, the attractiveness of any company often lies in its capacity to provide learning and experience. By this calculus, access to training, mentors, and challenging projects is more important than pay or benefits. Some prominent companies—General Electric, for example—have always been able to attract top talent, even when they could not promise upward mobility, because people see them as a training ground, a good place to learn, and a valuable addition to a résumé.

Reputation Reputation is a key resource in professional careers, and the chance to enhance it can be an outstanding motivator. The professional's reliance on reputation stands in marked contrast to the bureaucrat's anonymity. Professionals have to make a name for themselves, while traditional corporate managers and employees stayed behind the scenes. Indeed, the accumulation of reputational "capital" provides not only an immediate ego boost but also the kind of publicity that can bring other rewards, even other job offers. Managers can enhance reputation—and improve motivation—by creating stars, by providing abundant public recognition and visible awards, by crediting the authors of innovation, by publicizing people outside their own departments, and by plugging people into organizational and professional networks.

The new, collaborative organization is predicated on a logic of flexible work assignments, not of fixed job responsibilities. To promote innovation and responsiveness, two of today's competitive imperatives, managers need to see this new organization as a cluster of activity sets, not as a rigid structure. The work of leadership in this new corporation will be to organize both sequential and synchronous projects of varying length and breadth, through which varying combinations of people will move, depending on the tasks, challenges, and opportunities facing the area and its partners at any given moment.

Leaders need to carve out projects with tangible accomplishments, milestones, and completion dates and then delegate responsibility for these projects to the people who flesh them out. Clearly delimited projects can counter overload by focusing effort and can provide short-term motivation when the fate of the long-term mission is uncertain. Project responsibility leads to ownership of the results and sometimes substitutes for other forms of reward. In companies where product development teams define and run their own projects, members commonly say that the greatest compensation they get is seeing the advertisements for their products. "Hey, that's mine! I did that!" one engineer told me he trumpeted to his family the first time he saw a commercial for his group's innovation.

This sense of ownership, along with a definite time frame, can spur higher levels of effort. Whenever people are engaged in creative or problem-solving projects that will have tangible results by deadline dates, they tend to come in at all hours, to think about the project in their spare time, to invest in it vast sums of physical and emotional energy. Knowing that the project will end and that completion will be an occasion for reward and recognition makes it possible to work much harder.

Leaders in the new organization do not lack motivational tools, but the tools are different from those of traditional corporate bureaucrats. The new rewards are based not on status but on contribution, and they consist not of regular promotion and automatic pay raises but of excitement about mission and a share of the glory and the gains of success. The new security is not employment security (a guaranteed job no matter what) but *employability* security—increased value in the internal and external labor markets. Commitment to the organization still matters, but today managers build commitment by offering project opportunities. The new loyalty is not to the boss or to the company but to projects that actualize a mission and offer challenge, growth, and credit for results.

The old bases of managerial authority are eroding, and new tools of leadership are taking their place. Managers whose power derived from hierarchy and who were accustomed to a limited area of personal control are learning to shift their perspectives and widen their horizons. The new managerial work consists of looking outside a defined area of responsibility to sense opportunities and of forming project teams drawn from any relevant sphere to address them. It involves communication and collaboration across functions, across divisions, and across companies whose activities and resources overlap. Thus rank, title, or official charter will be less important factors in success at the new managerial work than having the knowledge, skills, and sensitivity to mobilize people and motivate them to do their best.

Information Technology and Tomorrow's Manager

Lynda M. Applegate, James I. Cash, Jr., and D. Quinn Mills

The year is 1958. It's a time of prosperity, productivity, and industrial growth for U.S. corporations, which dominate the world economy. Organizations are growing bigger and more complex by the day. Transatlantic cable service, which has just been initiated, and advances in transportation are allowing companies to expand into international markets. To handle the growth, companies are decentralizing decision making. To keep track of these burgeoning operations, they are hiring middle managers in droves. In fact, for the first time ever, white-collar workers outnumber blue-collar workers. Large companies are installing their first computers to automate routine clerical and production tasks, and "participatory management" is the buzzword.

It's also the year Harold J. Leavitt and Thomas L. Whisler predicted what corporate life would be like 30 years later. Their article "Management in the 1980s" (HBR November-December 1958) and its predictions ran counter to the trends that were then underway. Leavitt and Whisler said, for instance, that by the late 1980s, the combination of management science and information technology would cause middle-management ranks to shrink, top management to take on more of the creative functions, and large organizations to centralize again. Through the 1960s, 1970s, and early 1980s, Leavitt and Whisler's predictions met strong criticism. But as the 1980s draw to a close, they don't seem so farfetched. Instead, they seem downright visionary.

Downsizing and "flattening" have been common in recent years. One estimate has it that organizations have shed more than one million managers and staff professionals since 1979. As companies have reduced the number of middle managers, senior managers have increased their span of control and assumed additional responsibilities. Consider these two examples:

Within weeks after a comprehensive restructuring thinned management by 40%, the president of a large oil company requested an improved management control system for his newly appointed senior management team. In response, a sophisticated, on-line executive information system was developed. It did the work of scores of analysts and mid-level managers whose responsibilities had been to produce charts and graphs, communicate this information, and coordinate operations with others in the company. The president also mandated the use of electronic mail to streamline communication throughout the business.

A large manufacturing company recently undertook a massive restructuring to cut the cost and time required to bring a new product to market. The effort included layoffs, divestitures, and early retirements, which thinned middle management by 30%. The company adopted a sophisticated telecommunications network, which linked all parts of the multinational company, and a centralized corporate data base, which integrated all aspects of the highly decentralized business. Senior managers used the data base and networks to summarize and display data from inside and outside the company and to signal to employees the kinds of things they should focus on.

Information technology, which had once been a tool for organizational expansion, has become a tool for downsizing and restructuring. Both these companies used technology to improve centralized control and to create new information channels. But this improved centralized control did not come at the expense of decentralized decision making. In fact, the need to be responsive led to even more decentralized decision making. The companies reduced the number of middle managers, and the computer systems assumed many of the communication, coordination, and control functions that middle managers previously performed. The line managers who remained were liberated from some routine tasks and had more responsibility.

These effects are similar to what Leavitt and Whisler predicted. Taking their clues from the management science and technology research of the 1950s, Leavitt and Whisler contemplated how technology would influence the shape and nature of the organization. They understood that technology would enable senior management to monitor and control large organizations more effectively and that fewer middle managers would be needed to analyze and relay information. They did not anticipate, however, that microcomputers would enable simultaneous improvement in decentralized decision making.

In the past, managers had to choose between a centralized and a decentralized structure. Today there is a third option: technology-driven control systems that support the flexibility and responsiveness of a decentralized organization as well as the integration and control of a centralized organization.

What next?

Now that this wave of information technology has worked its way into practice, it's time to think about where we're headed next. When we turn to research to see what technical breakthroughs are on the horizon, as Leavitt and Whisler did, we find that the horizon itself has changed. It's now much closer. Since the 1950s, development time has been cut in half. What once took 30 years to get from pure research to commercial application now takes only 10 to 15.

Moreover, when earlier generations of technology were commercialized, managers tended to adopt the technology first and then try to figure out what to do with the new information and how to cope with the organizational implications. But for many companies, that approach is now grossly inadequate. The new technology is more powerful, more diverse, and increasingly entwined with the organization's critical business processes. Continuing to merely react to new technology and the organizational change it triggers could throw a business into a tailspin.

At the same time, the business environment is changing ever faster, and organizations must be more responsive to it. Yet certain facts of life restrain them from doing so. Companies want to be more flexible, yet job descriptions, compensation schemes, and control mechanisms are rigid. They want to use their resources effectively, yet it's not always clear who can contribute most to a project, especially among people in different functional areas. They want to be productive, but every time an employee goes to another company, a little bit of corporate history and experience walks out the door.

With the help of technology, managers will be able to overcome these problems and make their organizations far more responsive than they are today. We can look forward, in fact, to an era in which managers will do the shaping. Large organization or small, centralized or not—business leaders will have options they've never had before. The technology will be there to turn the vision into reality and to change it as circumstances evolve. With that in mind, making a next round of predictions and waiting to see if they come true seems too passive. It makes more sense to begin thinking about the kind of organization we want and taking the steps necessary to prepare for it.

We already see glimpses of the future in some progressive companies that have used technology creatively, but even they do not give us a complete picture of the kind of organization that will be possible—maybe even prevalent—in the twenty-first century. Some companies will choose to adopt a new organizational form that we call the "cluster organization."[1] By doing so, they will be able to run their large companies like small ones and achieve the benefits of both.

In the cluster organization, groups of people will work together to solve business problems or define a process and will then disband when the job is done. Team members may be geographically dispersed and unacquainted with each other, but information and communication systems will enable those with complementary skills to work together. The systems will help the teams carry out their activities and track the results of their decisions. Reporting relationships, control mechanisms, compensation schemes—all will be different in the cluster organization.

Technology will offer new options even to companies that don't wish to make all of the changes the cluster organization implies. The first step in understanding these options is to look, as Leavitt and Whisler did, at the technologies that will make them possible.

Tomorrow's machines

Much of the technology that will give managers the freedom to shape their organizations is already being commercialized—expert systems, group and cooperative work systems, and executive information systems. Expert and knowledge-based systems (a subset of artificial intelligence technology) are rapidly appearing in commercial settings. Every large company we've polled expects to have at least one production system using this technology by late 1989. Group and cooperative work systems have sprung up in a number of companies, primarily for use by multidisciplinary teams. Executive information systems, which track both internal and external information, enable senior managers to monitor and control large, geographically dispersed and complex organizations.

By the turn of the century, these and other technologies will be widely available. Companies will be able to pick and choose applications that fit their requirements. Computers will be faster, smaller, more reliable, and easier to use. They'll store vast amounts of information, and they'll be flexible enough to allow companies to change their information and communication systems as the environment changes.

In the twenty-first century, desktop computers will be as powerful as today's supercomputers, and supercomputers will run at speeds over a thousand times faster than today's. Computer chips now with one million processing elements will have more than one billion, and parallel processing (the ability to share a task among a number of processing units) will boost power tremendously.

It will be possible to communicate voluminous amounts of information in a variety of forms over long distances within seconds. Standard telephone lines and advanced cellular radio technology will provide access to high-speed networks that will whisk data, text, graphics, voice, and video information from one part of the world and send it to another instantly. Improved reliability and security will accompany the significantly higher network speeds and the improved performance.

Plugging all shapes and sizes of computers into tomorrow's network will be as easy as plugging in a telephone today. Telephones, in fact, will be replaced by computer phones that can convert speech into machine-readable text and can simultaneously transmit video images, voice, and data. Storing messages, transferring documents, paying bills, and shopping at home will all be possible through the same connection.

Computers the size of a small book will have the information processing power and storage capabilities of today's desktop workstations, yet will fit in a briefcase. They'll enable us to create and revise documents, review and answer mail, and even hold video conference meetings from anyplace that has a phone jack. Cellular terminals will allow even more freedom, since they won't require a wired telephone connection. And we will no longer be a slave to the keyboard; voice recognition technology will allow us to dictate messages and create and revise text as easily as using a dictaphone.

As computers become faster at processing and communicating information, we'll need better ways of storing and managing it. Optical storage media, similar to the compact-disk technology that is used today to store music, will hold much more information than is possible today and will retrieve information much more quickly.

And no longer will it be necessary to store data in static data bases that must be reprogrammed every time the business changes. Flexible, dynamic information networks called associative networks will do away with these rigid systems. Associative networks will allow us to store and manipulate information in a manner similar to the way we think. They will store data, voice, video, text, and graphics—but beyond that, they will store the relationships between information elements. As needs change and the network is reconfigured, the relationships among the data remain intact. Primitive associative information systems, used primarily to process large-text data bases (e.g., hypertext), are currently on the market. We can expect significant enhancements to these associative information systems in the next several years.

Tomorrow's computers will truly be more intelligent. Today's computers are designed to process information sequentially, one

Human factors: The gap between humans and machines

The most advanced fighter plane the United States has, the F-16, can perform without structural damage at a remarkable 12 times the force of gravity—12 G's. Since its introduction more than a decade ago, several dozen Air Force pilots have died flying the F-16, because even the best pilots with the best training and the best equipment can function at no more than 9 G's. That 3-G difference is what psychologists call "human factors"—the gap between human and machine capabilities.

As advanced technologies become increasingly pervasive in the workplace, the problem of human factors will increasingly confront managers. The fact that few managers have even heard of human factors—let alone thought of how to deal with them—is cause for great concern. . . .

In offices, the most troubling manifestation of the human factors problem has to do with information. Machines can now give us more information more quickly than we can possibly absorb it. There is no possibility of understanding all the information or of utilizing it effectively.

Food companies, for example, used to get market information monthly. Now they get it weekly, and marketing people are still struggling to process one week's information and make the right decisions based on it when the next week's information arrives. Before long, they will be receiving that information daily, and the prospect fills them with dread. Yet, they cannot avoid getting it, because they fear appearing to do less than their competitors.

We are in the grip of a seemingly irresistible technological imperative that, in effect, says, "Go, at all costs, go." But we must pause and think about what we really need and whether available technology can help us get what we need. . . .

Supporting intelligence rather than information gathering

Information (or data) is a raw material. Like iron, it must be transformed into something else before it can be used. Just as an automobile manufacturer cannot make a car without first converting iron to steel, managers cannot effectively make decisions without first transforming information into intelligence. The technology we now have is, in the main, information technology, not intelligence technology. Improvements in the technology are largely in its ability to gather, store, and catalog information. The promise of artificial intelligence remains remote.

What managers need is not information but intelligence. The *cri*

command at a time. This capability works well if the problem or task is structured and can be broken down into a series of steps. It doesn't work well for complex, unstructured tasks involving insight, creativity, and judgment. "Neural network" computers will change that.

de coeur from managers is "give us what we need to do our jobs better." Instead, they are inundated with data, and as a consequence they dawdle or delay, or they make decisions of which they themselves are dubious. Morale plummets, and what may be an instinctive fear of technology develops into the newest occupational illness, "techno-stress."

In fact, office technology has had no discernible positive impact on decision making. Ten years ago, 90–95% of new package goods introduced failed. Today—with an incredible increase in sophisticated machinery available to assist in product development and design and market analysis—90–95% of new products introduced still fail. . . .

Examining what technology can—and cannot—do It is first necessary to understand that in the management of organizations there is not yet a satisfactory substitute for human intelligence. It is then necessary to examine what technology can do to provide support for that crucial element—or how it might interfere. Only then can we have a proper context for the purchase and application of technology intended for use in the management of resources, people, and organizations.

As modest as these steps may seem, it is imperative that they be institutionalized before technology advances much further and, like Frankenstein's monster, becomes completely uncontrollable. Harvard physics professor Gerald Holton warns that the relentless advance of technological development puts even highly educated people at risk of becoming to some extent functionally illiterate. Holton calls this a "diminution of national possibility." Organizationally, it can mean management that is either impotent or increasingly irrational.

It is not a question of whether management can resist the technological imperative. It must. But how? The answer lies in employing more of what managers have been told is lacking in other aspects of business these days: creativity and innovation. . . .

Managers in growing numbers are asking questions about the effective utilization of technology. There now appears to be a pause in what was for a while a pell-mell rush to introduce technology throughout the workplace. Before proceeding, managers would be well advised to examine not only the technology but how it fits with people.

Source: Excerpted from Edith Weiner and Arnold Brown, "Human Factors: The Gap between Humans and Machine." Reprinted, with permission, from THE FUTURIST, published by the World Future Society, 4916 Saint Elmo Avenue, Bethesda, Maryland 20814.

Rather than processing commands one at a time, a neural network computer uses associative reasoning to store information as patterns of connections among millions of tiny processors, all of which are linked together. These computers attempt to mimic the actions of the human brain. When faced with a new pattern, the computer follows rules of logic to ask questions that help it figure out what to do with the anomaly.

Prototypes of neural network computers already exist. One group of researchers developed a neural network computer that contained the logic to understand English phonetics. The researchers gave the computer typed transcripts, containing 1,024 words, from a child in first grade, and it proceeded to read out loud. A human instructor "told" the computer each time it made a mistake, and within ten tries, the computer was reading the text in an understandable way. Within 50 tries, the computer was reading at 95% accuracy. No software programming was ever done.[2] The computer learned to read in much the same way that humans do.

We can also expect that by the twenty-first century there will be many companies that routinely use expert systems and other artificial intelligence applications. Knowledge bases, in which expertise is stored along with information, will become as commonplace as data bases are today. Technology will increasingly help people perform tasks requiring judgment and expert knowledge. Already, fighter aircraft technology is moving toward having the plane respond to what the pilot is thinking rather than his physical movements.

This type of technology will no longer simply make things more efficient; instead, the computer will become a tool for creativity, discovery, and education. Interactive technology based on optical storage is currently used in flight simulators to help pilots learn to make decisions. Some companies are experimenting with similar systems, described as digital video interactive, to help planners, analysts, researchers, functional specialists, and managers learn to make decisions without the risk and time associated with traditional experiential learning. These should help managers learn to be effective much more quickly.

Technologies will be well developed to meet the needs of senior executives. Sophisticated analytical, graphic, and computer interface capabilities will be able to aggregate, integrate, and present data in flexible and easy-to-use formats. Computers and special software will support executive planning, decision making, communication, and control activities. Some executives already use these applications to manage their businesses.

While in the past computers primarily supported individual work, the computer systems of the future will also be geared toward groups. Research on computer support for cooperative work has gained momentum over the past five years, and many companies are developing promising new technologies. Several companies are installing automated meeting rooms, and a number of vendors are working on software to support group activities. Researchers are now testing electronic brainstorming, group consensus, and negotiation software, and general meeting support systems. To help geographically dispersed group members work together, some companies are developing electronic communication software and applications that make communication and the exchange of documents and ideas faster and easier. These applications will allow skills to be better allocated.

The structure, the process, and the people

These and other advanced technologies will give managers a whole new set of options for structuring and operating their businesses. In the twenty-first century, like today, some companies will be small, some will be large; some will be decentralized, others will not. But technology will enable new organizational structures and management processes to spring up around the familiar ones, and the business world will be a very different place as a result. Here we describe the organizational structures, management processes, and human resource management strategies associated with the cluster organization and how the technology will make them possible in years to come.

Organizational structure:
Companies will have the benefits of small scale and large scale simultaneously.

Even large organizations will be able to adopt more flexible and dynamic structures.

The distinctions between centralized and decentralized control will blur.

The focus will be on projects and processes rather than on tasks and standard procedures.

The hierarchy and the matrix are the most common formal organization designs for large companies today. They structure communication, responsibility, and accountability to help reduce complexity and provide stability. But, as implemented today, they also tend to stifle innovation. With the environment changing as quickly as it does, the challenge has been to make large companies, with their economies of scale and other size advantages, as responsive as small ones.

Small companies, of course, have fewer layers of management and less bureaucracy, so the organization is less rigid. They adapt more easily to change and allow for creativity. Leadership and control are generally easier in small businesses because top management can communicate directly with workers and can readily trace the contribution individuals make. Information is also easier to track. Much of the knowledge is in people's heads, and everyone knows who to go to for expertise on a particular subject. People often have a chance to get involved with a broad range of responsibilities and therefore have a better understanding of the business as a whole.

These small organizations, especially those that are information-intensive and have a large percentage of professional employees, tend to be structured differently. We have termed the most fluid and flexible forms "cluster." Other authors talk of a network organization or an adhocracy.[3] In the network organization, rigid hierarchies are replaced by formal and informal communication networks that connect all parts of the company. In the adhocracy, a set of project-oriented work groups replace the hierarchy. Both of these forms are well known for their flexibility and adaptiveness. The Manned Space Flight Center of NASA, an example of an adhocracy, changed its organizational structure 17 times in the first 8 years of its existence.[4]

In what will be an even faster changing world than the one we now know, businesses of all sizes will need the ability to adapt to the dynamics of the external environment. Automated information and communication networks will support the sharing of information throughout a large, widely dispersed, complex company. The systems will form the organization's infrastructure and change the role of formal reporting procedures. Even in large corporations, each individual will be able to communicate with any other—just as if he or she worked in a small company.

The technologies that will allow these more fluid organizational forms are already coming into use in the form of electronic mail, voice mail, fax, data networks, and computer and video conferencing. Speed and performance improvements will collapse the time and distance that now separate people who could benefit from working together. The large organizations of the future will seem as tightly connected as small ones.

Computers will also help identify who in the company has the expertise needed to work on a particular problem. Databases of employees' skills and backgrounds will ensure that the mix of talent can be tailor-made for every task that arises. The systems will keep track of who knows what, and how to prepare an individual for the next project.

Managers in large companies will also have technological help in keeping track of where information resides and how to analyze it. Associative information networks and neural network computers will preserve the relationships among data elements and will store and manage information in a manner similar to the way we think. They will provide concise snapshots of the vast activities and resources of a large corporation. This will prevent managers from being overwhelmed by the scale and complexity.

Executives and senior managers will be less insulated from operations because executive information systems will help them get the information they need to monitor, coordinate, and control their businesses. Rather than waiting for the analysts and middle managers to prepare reports at the end of a prolonged reporting period, executives will have immediate access to information. Software will help do the analysis and present it in a usable format. With such immediate feedback, managers will be able to adjust their strategy and tactics as circumstances evolve rather than at fixed time intervals. And if a change in tactics or strategy is warranted, advanced communication technology will send the message to employees promptly.

Top management's ability to know what is going on throughout the organization won't automatically lead to centralization. With feedback on operations readily available at the top, the rigid policies and procedures that now aim to keep line managers on track can be relaxed. The systems will also liberate business managers by giving them the information and analytic support they need to make decisions and control their operations. Individuals and project teams will be able to operate fairly autonomously while senior management monitors the overall effects of their actions by the hour or day.

Most of the day-to-day activity will be project oriented. Because circumstances will change even faster than they do now, no two situations will be exactly alike or call for the same set of experts or procedures. The employees' skills and the approach will vary with the task at hand, so teams of people will form around particular projects and subsequently dissolve. Most responsibilities, then, will be handed over to project managers. Associative information networks will help those managers deploy resources, and software specially designed to support group work will aid communication, decision making, and consensus reaching. People who work together only infrequently will have the tools they need to be at least as effective as the permanent management team in a small company.

Management processes:
Decision making will be better understood.

Control will be separate from reporting relationships.

Computers will support creativity at all organizational levels.

Information and communication systems will retain corporate history, experience, and expertise.

Decision making is not well understood in most organizations. Managers often make choices based on thought processes they themselves cannot explain. They gather the information they think is relevant and reach what seems like the best conclusion. In the future, sophisticated expert systems and knowledge bases will help to capture those decision-making processes. Companies can then analyze and improve them.

As the decision processes become more explicit and well-defined and as companies learn what information is required, the level of the person making the decision becomes less important. It will still be important to monitor the outcome and to make sure the circumstances surrounding the decision haven't completely changed.

Management control is now exerted through the formal organizational chart. A manager at a given level in the organization is responsible for everything that happens below that level. That same person channels information up through the organization to the person he or she reports to.

But when technology allows top management to monitor data at the lowest organizational level without the help of intermediaries and when employees at all levels and in all functions can communicate directly, formal control systems do not have to be embedded in organizational reporting relationships. The ability to separate control from reporting relationships means that both systems can be handled most effectively. For instance, top management can exercise control directly by monitoring results at all levels, while a different set of relationships exists for reporting purposes. These reporting relationships would focus on employee motivation, creativity, and socialization.

By doing a lot of the analytical work, expert systems and artificial intelligence tools will free up workers at all levels to be more creative. Up to now, only top management jobs have been structured to allow as much time as possible for creative thinking. As technology helps managers with coordination, control, decision making, and communication, they too will have the time and encouragement to make discoveries and use the new resources innovatively.

The transience of even specialized workers won't be nearly the problem in the twenty-first century that it is today. Information systems will maintain the corporate history, experience, and expertise that long-time employees now hold. The information systems themselves—not the people—can become the stable structure of the organization. People will be free to come and go, but the value of their experience will be incorporated in the systems that will help them and their successors run the business.

In this environment, companies will need fewer managers. Those managers that do assume executive positions, however, will lack the experiential learning acquired through years as a middle manager. Their career paths will not take them through positions of increasing responsibility where they oversee the work of others. Executive information systems will enable them to "get up to speed" quickly on all parts of the business. Sophisticated business analysis and simulation models will help them analyze business situations and recognize the consequences, thereby decreasing and managing risk.

Human resources:
Workers will be better trained, more autonomous, and more transient.

The work environment will be exciting and engaging.

Management will be for some people a part-time activity that is shared and rotated.

Job descriptions tied to narrowly defined tasks will become obsolete.

Compensation will be tied more directly to contribution.

In the 1950s and 1960s, computers took on many operational and routine tasks. In the 1970s and 1980s, they assumed some middle-management decision-making, coordinating, and controlling tasks. As the technology affects even more aspects of the business, work itself will change and require a different set of skills. People will need to be technically sophisticated and better educated in order to cope with the demands on them. Employees must be capable of leading—rather than being led by—the technology, capable of using technology as a lever against the increased complexity and pace of change in their business environments.

As top management seizes on its ability to monitor without restricting freedom, employees will have more control over their own work. There will be fewer rigid policies from a less visible headquarters. Also, as the nature of the work changes from implementing a particular company's standard operating procedures to participating in a series of projects that call on one's expertise, workers will be less tied to any one organization, and building loyalty to a company will be harder than it is today. In some companies, loyalty may be less critical than having access to the skills a given employee has to offer. As companies pull together the resources they need on a project-by-project basis and as information and communication networks extend beyond the organization, company boundaries will be harder to define. Organizations may draw on expertise that lies in a supplier or an independent consultant if appropriate.

Because workers will be highly skilled and the organization will offer fewer opportunities for advancement, employees will expect the work environment to be rewarding. If they are not stimulated or if their independence is threatened, they will go elsewhere.

In these ways, companies of the future will closely resemble professional service firms today. The most successful firms attract and retain employees by providing an environment that is intellectually engaging. The work is challenging, the projects diverse, and the relationships with clients fairly independent. Some professionals work with more than one firm—like doctors who admit patients to several hospitals.

Management will be a part-time job as group members share responsibility and rotate leadership. Except at the top of the organization, there will be few jobs that consist solely of overseeing the work of others—and then primarily for measurement and control purposes. Each work group may have a different leader. In addition, the leadership of a single group may rotate among members, depending on what the business problem requires. Employees will take on a management role for short periods, and as a result, will have a better understanding of the entire business.

Detailed, task-oriented job descriptions will be less important because the job will be changing all the time. In a sense, everyone will be doing the same job—lending their special skills and expertise to one project after another. In another sense, every job will be unique—people with different kinds of expertise will work on different sets of projects. Information systems will be able to account for the work each person does and the skills and experience he or she possesses.

The ability to track each individual's skill and participation in the company outside the traditional organizational forms creates a whole new freedom: the ability to pay each person for his or her actual contribution to the organization without upsetting an entire pay scale or hierarchical structure. Currently, if the company wants to create an incentive for a particular person, it is often constrained by the compensation system itself. To raise one person's salary requires boosting everyone else above that point in the hierarchy.

Flexible, dynamic compensation packages will allow companies to treat individuals as unique contributors and to reward them based on their particular skills. In some companies, an employee's compensation may follow the pattern of a normal distribution curve, matching the employee's desired work pattern and contribution to the company. Salaries would increase and peak between ages 40 and 50, and then decline.

Be creative but be careful

The new technologies hold great promise that our large, rigid hierarchies will become more adaptive, responsive, and better suited to the fast-paced world of the twenty-first century. But these technologies do not come without risk. Processing information faster may seem like a good idea, but it is possible to process information too fast. As speed increases, efficiency of a process improves only to a point. That point is reached when it is no longer possible to monitor and control the results of the process. Beyond that point, the process of collecting information, making decisions, monitoring feedback, and evaluating performance breaks down. The experience of some companies during the stock market crash of October 19, 1987 shows what can happen when information is processed faster than we can monitor and control it.

There are also risks associated with integrating data from diverse sources. For one thing, we run the risk of data overload, in which case people unable to understand or use the information and the tools that convert data into information may fail. Also, the creation of integrated data bases may lead to unintended liabilities. For example, when an elevator manufacturer created a centralized service and repair center, it also created a legal liability. A large, centralized data base containing the maintenance and repair records of all of their elevators in North America provided an attractive target for subpoena by any suitor.

Computerization of critical business processes may also create security risks. Sabotage, fraud, record falsification, and theft become more threatening than ever. And with more information stored electronically, privacy issues become more acute.

Leavitt and Whisler were wise to believe that information technology would influence the structure of organizations, their management processes, and the nature of managerial work. Our 30-year history of information technology use in organizations suggests that in the future managers must be much more actively involved in directing technology and managing its influence on organizations.

Technology will not be an easy solution to serious problems and it won't guarantee competitiveness. As always, it will require thoughtful planning and responsible management. But as never before, it will tax the creative powers of the business leaders who must decide when to use it—and to what end.

1. See D. Quinn Mills, *The Rebirth of the Corporation* (New York: John Wiley and Sons, 1990).

2. Terrence Sejnowski and Charles Rosenberg, "Parallel Networks That Learn to Pronounce English Text," *Complex Systems* 1 (1987): 145.

3. See Robert G. Eccles and Dwight B. Crane, "Managing through Networks in Investment Banking," *California Management Review* (Fall 1987): 176;

and Henry Mintzberg, "The Adhocracy," in *The Strategy Process*, ed. James Brian Quinn, Henry Mintzberg, and Robert M. James (Englewood Cliffs, NJ: Prentice-Hall, 1988), 607.

4. As reported in Henry Mintzberg, *Structuring in Fives: Designing Effective Organizations* (Englewood Cliffs, NJ: Prentice-Hall, 1983).

PART 4

Governance: What's Next?

Foresight: Addressing Tomorrow's Problems Today

Lindsey Grant

Everybody talks about the weather, but nobody does anything about it.
—Mark Twain

Perhaps the time has come to tell Mark Twain that we are finally doing something about the weather. Not exactly what we had anticipated. In fact, we didn't anticipate anything at all, and that perhaps is a good beginning for a proposal about foresight.

The human tribe can now perturb the planet. We are even developing sophisticated processes to monitor what we are doing to the earth. The next question—and the one that is not yet answered—is, "How are we going to organize that knowledge and make use of it?"

The problems that face the U.S. government are interconnected, but the government's decision-making machinery is not. There is a pressing need for new decision-making machinery—institutions of foresight—to deal with a world whose complexity has swamped the government's existing decision processes.

"Foresight" is a systematic, institutionalized process for (1) looking ahead to identify issues that the government should be addressing, and for (2) bringing all available perspectives together, so that the ramifications of a proposed policy can be considered before a decision is made. Foresight requires that the different components of government be able to communicate, with mutually understood terminology and definitions and with assumptions and thought processes spelled out for others to understand.

The need to deal with a changing world is becoming a political question. People are beginning to wonder what the government is going to do about such problems as:

Sewage sludge and hospital garbage on the beach

Mountains denuded by some mysterious combination of acid precipitation and ozone

Rising sea levels and world temperatures that are climbing because of the greenhouse effect

An ozone hole over Antarctica created by chlorofluorocarbons, which also contribute to the greenhouse effect, causing a loss of stratospheric ozone that may affect things as diverse as human skin-cancer rates and the oceanic food chain.

The multiple implications of human activities

The United States and the world are paying already for the failure to consider the implications of human activities:

The population of the Third World would be less by perhaps a billion people if government leaders in the 1950s—when the assault on disease and high mortality was begun—had considered what would happen if mortality were reduced without reducing fertility. The problem is now being attacked a generation later under much less favorable circumstances.

The Department of Energy estimates that it will cost the United States $66–$100 billion to clean up and dismantle obsolete or reduced nuclear weapons stockpiles. If the cleanup had been built into the nuclear-weapons program, the country would not be facing this bill.

The United States left hazardous-waste disposal largely unregulated until a decade ago. A $10-billion "Superfund" was authorized by Congress to deal with the results, but estimates of the cost of cleaning up the worst problem sites range from $23 billion to $100 billion, and nobody pretends to know how many dangerous sites remain undiscovered. An earlier focus on the byproducts of chemical production would have saved these catch-up costs.

The Environmental Protection Agency (EPA) estimates that one-third of the 796,000 underground fuel tanks in the United States are leaking, posing a threat to the nation's aquifers. Once the pollutants start migrating through the earth toward the aquifers, there is no way of catching up with them; one must simply learn to deal with poisoned water. Better construction standards and the registration of tanks—both now required—would have avoided that disastrous outcome.

Such problems are multiplying. They often can be dealt with in advance, sometimes at very little cost. But hindsight is of little help.

The EPA is attempting to enforce a miscellany of laws intended to control air, water, and soil pollution. These laws are inconsistent and sometimes contradictory. Only a few of them take into account the economic and social implications of their enforcement. The time has come for a better way of making such decisions.

Crossing departmental lines

Government needs to look farther ahead than it is accustomed, to examine the side effects of proposed policies, to avoid the blind alleys, and to see the opportunities. Issues as diverse as world climate and American international competitiveness ride on the improvement of national foresight capability.

Problems cross departmental lines and so do solutions, but each department and agency identifies its problems and seeks solutions within its own framework, in isolation from others.

For example, the government's acid-rain policy is being set by a committee that does not include representatives from the Department of Housing and Urban Development or the Department of Transportation. Yet, any successful attack on acid rain will probably require changes in urban residential and transportation patterns. Meanwhile, the Department of Transportation tries to put off the specter of gridlock by studying proposals for ever-vaster highways —even though highway traffic is a principal source of the atmospheric pollution that causes acid rain.

The destruction of tropical forests is a major contributor to the greenhouse effect and the principal reason for the current decline in genetic diversity. A major cause of this forest loss is Third World population growth. Yet, none of the solutions to tropical-forest loss proposed by governmental or international bodies includes any effort to deal with that source of the problem. Agency for International Development (AID) budgets for population programs have been declining for years. None of the experts proposed that priorities within the AID budget be looked at again. It is not their department.

The Department of Energy, in a recent long-term assessment, identified U.S. population growth as a source of rising energy demands. It took note of the investment and environmental problems associated with increasing energy capacity, but it did not consider whether a population policy would contribute to addressing the problems.

There is no interdepartmental group looking at the implications of the coming transition from petroleum to other energy sources. After the first "energy crisis," President Nixon attempted a quick fix: "Project Independence," a proposal to reduce American dependence on foreign oil. But in an economy that has been built on petroleum, the adjustment away from it will not be so simple.

Everything from agriculture to transportation to recreational habits will be influenced by the changing mix and rising cost of energy. The transition is not just a problem; it is an opportunity to address environmental stresses such as acid rain, the greenhouse effect, and water pollution. But it will require thinking from a number of perspectives.

Foresight should focus not only on the problems ahead, but also on the opportunities. Foresight applied to genetic research, for instance, might suggest where the biggest payoffs lie. Nitrogen fixation in food grains might save the ecological and economic costs of commercial fertilizers and reduce the pollution of bodies of water such as the Chesapeake Bay. And bacteriological transformation might be a promising way to deal with toxic chemical wastes.

A new way of seeing

Government does not have a monopoly on tunnel vision. It pervades human thinking. Foresight calls for a new approach to thinking, a recognition that things are interconnected, not just conceptually but vitally; that one mind or discipline cannot understand all the connections; that interdisciplinary communication is essential to clear thinking in this new and complex world.

Old habits die hard. At least two presidents of the American Association for the Advancement of Science have called for a new emphasis on interdisciplinary thinking. The editor of *Science* magazine has made an explicit connection between human population growth, species diversity, and the future of life on the planet, with the impassioned plea that we "curb our primordial instinct to increase replication of our own species at the expense of others because the global ecology is threatened. So ask not whether the bell tolls for the owl or the whale or the rhinoceros; it tolls for us."

If we judge from the pages of *Science,* such advice has had little effect on scientists' parochialism. In articles on protecting tropical forests, on dealing with the greenhouse effect and acid precipitation, on curbing the loss of genetic diversity, or on revising energy policy, one reads all sorts of proposals for technical fixes but no hint that population policies could have a role in solving the problems. Scientific specialization seems to narrow one's perspectives.

The only true current application of foresight that comes to mind—a proposal to make changes in one sector to effect improvement in another—is the National Energy Policy Act, introduced in the U.S. Senate by Timothy Wirth, senator from Colorado, which would hold down the increase in U.S. energy consumption to ameliorate the greenhouse effect. To do so, it proposes redirecting U.S. aid toward forestry and population programs.

There is another way in which foresight, properly applied, could promote a fundamental change in thinking processes. Foresight helps focus decision makers' attention on the consequences of policies rather than on emotional responses or preconceptions. The immigration issue is a good case in point. It is a value-laden, emotion-ridden topic. It can also be examined from the perspective of consequences.

Immigration currently accounts for perhaps one-third to one-half of U.S. population growth. Population experts do not know exactly, because there are no good estimates of illegal immigration. The debate so far has been conducted primarily in moral generalizations, but immigration policy affects most departments and many national objectives: energy use, urban infrastructure, social services, education, unemployment, the supply of certain skills such as nurses and doctors, health and epidemic strategies, even drug control. Few of the potentially concerned agencies such as the Department of Labor played a role in shaping immigration policy. The administration should have an immigration-foresight group, looking at the implications of different immigration policies in terms of their relevance to all those national interests.

A present and future case: Los Angeles

Immigration leads us (as it does many immigrants) to California. That state, and particularly the Los Angeles area, is the fastest-growing state in the United States and the chief destination of immigrants. The area is, geologically, the collision zone where the Pacific continental plate is grinding its way northward against the North American plate. The state is mostly desert, and already its demand for water is upsetting ecological balances throughout the region. California pipes in its water and much of its petroleum and gas and trucks in its food supplies across the nation's most active geological fault zone—the San Andreas fault—and so is extremely vulnerable.

Given this combination of circumstances, Los Angeles provides a good example of the uses of foresight. It it were politically possible—which it currently is not—there are some serious questions that should be asked.

The U.S. Geological Survey Working Group on California Earthquake Possibilities believes that there is a 60-70% chance of a major earthquake somewhere on the southern San Andreas fault within the next 30 years. There are more than 13 million people in the greater Los Angeles metropolitan area. A recent "moderate" earthquake in Whittier—less than one-tenth as severe as the lower limit of the projected major earthquake—caused $350 million in damages. One can imagine a very grim scenario indeed in the case of a major earthquake.

Should the government not be considering a more restrictive view of immigration, if the majority of immigrants tend to head for Los Angeles?

Even more fundamentally, should it be national policy to discourage the further growth of that vulnerable area? With much less at stake, the United States decided in 1982 to stop encouraging development on the Atlantic and Gulf barrier islands by suspending federal subsidies for new flood insurance, roads, buildings, and housing. Should a foresight task force be looking at the much graver problem in California? There is little doubt that the federal government will shoulder much of the cost if there is a disaster.

Mobilizing to protect a shared planet

Foresight is not simply an insider's game. The decisions facing the United States may be painful. Acid rain provides a good example. It already poses a threat to the well-being of parts of the United States and Canada and to most of Europe. It threatens soil microorganisms and the entire food chain. Yet, if acid rain is to be controlled, the price will be very high. No government is going to be able to impose the needed economic changes unless the electorate understands the necessity and is willing to pay the price. The foresight process can help to develop that grass-roots support if it makes government more accessible to outsiders, if it identifies where in government to find those who are dealing with a problem, and if it thereby helps to promote an informed national debate about the choices a country faces.

Foresight also has an international aspect. The world beyond a country's borders affects that nation in a variety of ways, whether it be weather or acid rain or human migration or food and trade or the threat of war. Foresight can take into account such interactions, but that is only the first step. Nations must cooperate with other nations to obtain the data needed to understand what is happening.

Moreover, if nations use the foresight process together, they may develop a shared perspective of what needs to be done. Some problems can be resolved only if they are dealt with multilaterally. The joint pursuit of foresight may be integral to the larger effort of learning how to reconcile a system of sovereign states with the fact of a shared planet.

Prospects for foresight

There is widespread support for foresight. Most major U.S. environmental organizations are on record in favor of it. From a very different quarter, the Grace Commission—whose chairman, J. Peter Grace, is hardly regarded as friendly to environmentalists—made proposals for improving government foresight under the name of improved management. Foresight as an idea is not politically polarized.

Instituting foresight is a question of organization, not of funding, of bringing different perspectives together to focus on policy options rather than on creating new bureaucracies. Within the White House, the Domestic Policy, Economic Policy, and National Security Councils provide the framework for improved foresight.

The president of the United States must be involved if foresight is to be improved. He will need to designate a senior official in whom he has great confidence, whose sole responsibility would be to see that all the relevant perspectives are developed and brought into policy decisions and that the executive-branch agencies are brought into better communication with each other and with the outside world.

Most administrations organize themselves in the first two or three months and then become enmeshed in day-to-day crises. The president who can change the structures of government so that it can deal with wider horizons and the growing complexities of the modern world will have done something more. As the man who built the great chateau of Chenonceaux inscribed on his mantel: *Si ça va à point, me souviendra.* "If I carry it through, I will be remembered."

Prospects for State-Local Relations

Jane F. Roberts

Devolutionary and decentralizing trends, together with uncertain economic and fiscal conditions in many sections of the country, have posed major challenges to state and local policymakers in recent years. It has been a decade of substantial transition and adjustment for the intergovernmental system, unparalleled for many years in scope and significance. As the dust settles, state and local governments are responding to new challenges and retooling for substantial new responsibilities for financing and providing programs and services in an era of "do-it-yourself federalism."

Despite continuing serious concerns about federal tax policies and budget and trade deficit reductions, all of which have tremendous implications for the state-local sector, state and local officials (1) continue to place emphasis on traditional service-delivery and program responsibilities, (2) have taken the lead in a broad range of entrepreneurial activities, and (3) are demonstrating progress in forging stronger state-local partnerships. When viewed together, these developments provide hopeful signals that state and local governments are indeed responding to the challenges posed by a decentralizing federal system and an increasingly complex and internationalized fiscal order.

The fiscal landscape

The decade of the Eighties has been a period of upheaval for intergovernmental fiscal relations, and the prospects for the near future may be for more of the same. State fiscal conditions improved for many states in the past year, but most states expect to draw down

Reprinted with permission from *National Civic Review* (September-October 1989).

their reserves in the current year. According to the annual survey of state fiscal conditions of the National Conference of State Legislatures (NCSL), the greatest concentration of fiscal problems was in the New England states and in New York and New Jersey, places that just two years ago were faring better than most other states. As noted by NCSL President-elect Lee Daniels, minority leader of the Illinois House of Representatives: "The experience of the states in the early 1980s should instill caution. Even though many of the states are in good fiscal condition, the current balances are really much less than states held in 1980, when inflation and the growth of state budgets are considered. Current fiscal health is certainly not cause for complacency."

State fiscal conditions   According to the NCSL survey, 41 states made noteworthy tax changes during the year, with tax increases in 30 states and decreases in 11 states. Excise taxes were the most common taxes increased, with 23 states raising motor fuel taxes, 13 increasing cigarette taxes, and seven boosting alcoholic beverage levies. The main tax cuts were broad personal income tax reductions in six states. As in most years, education was identified as the leading fiscal issue. It was followed closely by taxation. General budget policy, the third leading issue, was not mentioned as often as in previous years because of the healthy condition of most state budgets. The survey also suggests that pressure on state budgets has its origin in increased costs of providing services rather than in absolute declines in expected revenues. Increased needs in the areas of primary education, health care, and Medicaid topped most state agendas this past year. Additionally, unfunded federal mandates have been more of a problem for states recently than federal aid cutbacks, adding billions of dollars per year of new responsibilities. As noted by Louisiana State Senator Samuel Nunez, president of the NCSL: "Federal initiatives in welfare reform, catastrophic health care and nursing home legislation together will increase state costs by more than $2 billion per year."

The local scene   By contrast, the local fiscal picture is one of building pressures. Despite substantial increases in local fees and taxes, cities throughout the country are experiencing severe budget pressures while contending with declining revenues. According to the National League of Cities' (NLC) annual study of local fiscal conditions, property tax rates went up by 41 percent; increased charges and fees for municipal services were imposed by 69 percent of the survey group; new taxes appeared in 10 percent of the localities; and new fees and charges were reported by 36 percent of the jurisdictions. The survey of 362 cities found that nearly half expected to see expenditures outpace revenues in 1989, compared to 36 percent in 1988, forcing them to draw from their reserve funds. A slowdown in the growth of local operating budgets was reported by 43 percent of the communities, while 36 percent made actual reductions in capital spending. In releasing the report, NLC executive director Alan Beals observed: "The burden is shifted, the taxes are shifted, and the cities get clobbered."

The public view   Local property taxes top the list as the "worst tax," according to a nationwide survey conducted by the Gallup Organization for the Advisory Commission on Intergovernmental Relations (ACIR). Almost one-third (32 percent) of the American public said that local property taxes are the worst tax; federal income taxes came in second (27 percent), followed by state sales taxes (18 percent) and state income taxes (10 percent). The current survey results mark the first time since 1977 that local property taxes were clearly perceived by the public to be the worst tax. In the decade 1978–1988, the federal income tax usually was ranked the worst, or tied with the property tax. The 1989 shift is especially interesting because the proportions of respondents selecting state income or sales taxes as the worst remained unchanged from 1988. It is possible, therefore, that the Federal Tax Reform Act of 1986 is having an impact on public opinion. At the same time, however, with declining federal aid and rising costs, many local governments are experiencing pressures to raise revenues. Taken together, changes in federal taxes and rising local revenue pressure may be contributing to the increased dissatisfaction with property taxes.

The ACIR poll also revealed that the public believes that (1) local officials are the "most honest," (2) local government spends tax dollars the most wisely and is most responsive to public needs, and (3) local governments need more power (a majority indicated that the federal government has too much power).

How officials see it

There are 50 diverse state-local delivery systems, and like it or not, state and local officials must work together to provide most services. State and local officials alike must understand and be sensitive to problems which others must confront in delivering services and programs, particularly since so many are shared problems.

One avenue to reach a better understanding is to measure the impact of state policies on local governments, and to document how local governments (and state officials as well) assess the "state" of state-local relations to better determine exactly where the friction points exist.

In 1987, an effort was undertaken by the New York Commission on State-Local Relations to quantify these perceptions and evaluate the state of state-local relations. State and local officials were asked

to rate funding and other means of support, procedural requirements, and relative levels of concern in a number of service areas; to
offer an opinion about the current overall state-local relationship;
and to indicate whether the state of affairs had improved or deterio-
rated over the past five years.

Not surprisingly, state officials felt that state-local relationships were in better shape than did local officials, and further, that
the relationship was improving (local officials again disagreed).
While the results did not reveal any major surprises, they did, nonetheless, begin to pinpoint the nature of some of the areas of dis-
agreement, and perhaps to put them into clearer perspective. Since
the pioneering effort was undertaken in New York, four other states
and one public interest group have administered similar surveys,
with similar results. These kinds of efforts to determine the nature,
cause and severity of frictions—as well as identify strengths and
improvements—bode well for gaining a better working relationship
between state governments and their local jurisdictions.

In matters of local governance

State actions to revise or extend local government structures, functions and fiscal authority are an important—if not key—element of
intergovernmental relations. Yet, most times, they are the most difficult to accomplish.

State ACIRs   State advisory commissions on intergovernmental
relations (ACIRs) and comparable organizations also have become
increasingly important vehicles for discussing and studying state-
local issues and for proposing solutions to statewide problems. Indi-
vidually, these organizations have very different characteristics,
but an important common factor is their recognition that the state-
local partnership must be nurtured.

When the national ACIR first called upon the states to create
their own commissions over a decade ago, there were only four
ACIRs in operation. In 1989, 29 states had an intergovernmental
counterpart agency, of which 27 were active. Nearly a dozen other
states had a state ACIR proposal under consideration or were seeking ways to restructure or otherwise strengthen their existing organizations.

State mandates   State mandating of local government services
and programs increasingly has become an irritant in state-local relations. While these mandates may be justified in many instances,
they raise distinctly intergovernmental issues centering on the division of authority and financing responsibility between state and local governments. Simply stated: mandates oftentimes substitute
state priorities for local priorities.

Few issues cause more concern among local officials than state (and federal) mandates. Yet despite widespread concern, little systematic data have been available about their imposition and real costs.

No new state mandate reimbursement programs were enacted during 1989, but there was appreciable progress in the willingness of state officials to address the issue and to consider alternatives.

Economic and community-development initiatives

State and local governments have long been involved in economic and industrial development. Obvious as the relationship is between government and business, actions during 1985–86 suggest that their interactions are continuing to change: government is going beyond its traditional supportive role and business decisions increasingly consider total impact on communities and states. The rhetoric of partnership is gradually turning into ongoing institutional behavior, less adversarial and more entrepreneurial.

Hard financial and economic skills, tough realism, and genuine creativity are being melded together to advance local economic growth. Past experiments have matured, and new ideas have moved from concept to start-up venture.

Recent years have witnessed an expansion into new directions. State and local governments still fund infrastructure projects, but now they also promote high technology and educational opportunities, apply new technologies to mature industries, provide the bulk of job training, support small businesses, and target their aid to distressed urban and rural communities.

This expansion results largely from two forces: the national government's retrenchment from large economic and community-development programs, and the increasing capacity and willingness of states to fill this vacuum. While state and local government initiatives play a relatively small role in the condition of the overall economy, their initiatives do create products, services, jobs, and revenues which aid and support the national economy.

New entrepreneurs During the past few years, states and localities have significantly expanded both the level and nature of their development efforts.

Two trends have emerged in the past few years. First, public officials have begun to confront such traditional issues as health, welfare and unemployment in fundamentally different ways. Rather than concentrating efforts on after-the-fact remedies, lawmakers are examining root causes and devising and implementing prevention strategies. Secondly, state and local governments are assuming entrepreneurial roles in their economies. They are examining such things as barriers to business formation, private investment, and job markets, and they are devising research and development strategies to maintain a competitive edge in an ever-expanding global economy. Public expenditures are now being viewed as investments to achieve not only immediate programmatic goals, but long-range revitalization as well.

State and local experimentation with less traditional alternatives and entrepreneurial investments has achieved a fairly impressive record to date. Recent surveys show that states are pursuing better information for industrial prospects, broader access to capital, and closer ties between research institutions, local governments, and the private sector.

Conclusion

Recent years have witnessed a further strengthening of a public conviction that state and local governments have come of age, and that the capacity is in place to build the foundations of workable communities and a workable society. With this growing maturity, states and localities are attempting to set priorities, attain consensus, and exploit opportunities for innovation which are inherent in a federal system. At the same time, the economic uncertainties in some regions of the country are not over. Nonetheless, the mood is one of resolve and responsibility: to get on with the public's business.

The intergovernmental sorting process will continue, and the responsibilities of governing in a more decentralized federal system will increase. That is both the challenge and context for state and local policymakers.

Metropolitan Governance Statement

National Civic League

The following statement on metropolitan governance was drafted by a National Civic League committee including Iowa State Representative Jack Hatch, syndicated columnist Neal Peirce, Phoenix Mayor Terry Goddard, and Curtis Johnson, executive director of the Citizens League in the Twin Cities. It was adopted by the Board of Directors of the National Civic League on October 29, 1989.

Life in urban America will decline seriously in the 1990s in the absence of dramatically improved metropolitan area-wide governance. No single municipality, however well governed, will be able to handle such mounting problems as traffic congestion, air pollution, inadequate mass transit, or solid and industrial waste. Nor can society's mounting social dilemmas—homelessness, inadequate housing, rising racism, the abandonment of children—be effectively addressed on anything less than a comprehensive, region-wide basis.

The successful regions of the next century will be those which learn to think of their entire metropolitan area as their community and take timely action to mobilize joint resources—governmental, corporate, foundation, academic—on a metropolitan-wide basis.

The need remains for well run, efficient local governments within each metropolitan area. For example, most if not all street maintenance, fire and community police services, codes and inspections, and detailed zoning decisions can be handled well by cities and towns.

But the "big" governance issues, from education to social services to major land-use patterns to assuring a quality work force for

the next century, demand a governing structure with true accountability on the truly regional issues. City leadership, beset with
shrinking tax bases, rising costs, and development forces playing
one municipality off against another, should not just welcome, but
demand, some effective regional rule-setting and governance.

The regions that make regionalism work will be those which position themselves for full human and economic development and compete more effectively in the international marketplace. Chambers of
commerce, for example, are learning that to work strategically and
effectively for economic development, their planning scope must en-
compass entire metropolitan regions. Critical governance decisions
need to be seen just as widely.

Formation of new, "pure" metropolitan governments is most
unlikely in today's politics. Americans repeatedly vote against
merging or disbanding their existing cities and towns.

But metropolitan areas require single area-wide authorities
that can be held accountable for drawing up policies and overseeing
services that are truly region-wide.

In some instances those area-wide authorities may be strengthened county governments. In other regions, where there are multiple counties, a common authority among the local governments
must be established.

Each region's history and political dynamics will influence the
type of metropolitan governance it develops. But to achieve accountability for the critical regional decisions, many regions may wish to
consider a directly elected council. Council membership, under such
an approach, could vary by at-large and direct election. An executive officer for the region could be chosen by the council from among
its members, or by separate direct election. He or she might be
called "regional executive" or "regional mayor."

Under the American system of 50 separate state governments
and hundreds of varying metropolitan forms, "many flowers" can
and should bloom as civic forces work to perfect the best and most
appropriate structures for their metropolitan future. Whatever
their precise form of government, all areas need to look less toward
treating problems on a piecemeal basis, and more toward a rational
sorting out of duties among the various local governments.

But there is no permanently satisfactory substitute for some
form of metropolitan governance which assures that the policies
critical for everyone's future—from adequate child care and education of our youth to environmentally safe recycling of our wastes to
rational land use—work in a quality, coordinated way, for the benefit of the whole region.

Special-purpose authorities in such areas as transit, waste water or job training might retain their operating authority, but all
should be ultimately responsible to a regional authority. Local

schools and universities need to be accountable, region-wide, in some way.

The driving force to gain popular and political support for shared and focused metropolitan governance must be citizen leagues, neighborhood and environmental coalitions, corporate

---

Memphis and the Mid-South Common Market:
An example of the future

To grow and prosper in the decade ahead we must find a way to pull the diverse resources and groups that define our communities into a process designed to foster full and successful participation in the global economy. The new reality, after all, has already made the traditional ideas of "national economies" and borders obsolete. We already have deep and growing involvement in the global economy throughout our communities through investors, foreign enterprises, exchange programs, etc. These occur independent of, and sometimes in spite of, any involvement by a nation—or even state—economic or political body.

But making our way forward and drawing fully on what is needed to create vibrant and excellent communities will be no simple task. Existing political bodies and boundaries, economic development institutions and basic measurement and reward systems get in the way of the type of cooperation we need to develop. The wave of the future, in fact, is in the development of regional innovations and enterprises that transcend everything currently in place.

The public and private leadership of Memphis, Tennessee, could easily move into the future with a rich array of plans and visions for the city with little regard for the surrounding area. It could easily position itself and its efforts to compete for status and recognition with Orlando, Nashville, Phoenix, Albuquerque, San Diego, etc. It has, instead, embarked on a different and bold route. It has decided to launch and support an effort that rests on the premise that the long-term health of Memphis is dependent upon the strength of the entire region—and the region is not among the strongest in any terms. Memphis has correctly recognized that a weak region will eventually lead to a weak city and, conversely, that business expansion in any part of the region is, in fact, good for the city regardless of the jurisdiction within which it occurs. Therefore, the goal is to make the region as strong and exciting as possible.

What is now underway is an effort termed the "Mid-South Common Market" that is designed to bring into a cooperative economic development venture 105 counties in 6 states! To accomplish this will require long, enthusiastic and visionary leadership because it runs

leaders, and community foundations. Only citizen power can set the political groundwork.

State authority for revised local governance will be a must. State legislatures need to recognize that effective regional decision making is a prerequisite if metropolitan areas are to be economi-

---

right into all the preconceived notions of who does and does not matter, who has power, who should be concerned about whom. It requires cooperation on all fronts.

Why bother? Among the very practical reasons for this effort are such realities as the first questions that are asked when prospective companies visit. While they used to be questions about "the city," they are now questions about "the region." Today's new factories, offices and research parks are more likely to be located in the "suburbs" or a small-town environment than in the center city. In the Mid-South region there are many such cities. Can they each offer everything they need to grow and to serve new business or industry needs? Alone, it is unlikely. Together, however, they are discovering that they can meet almost any perceived need.

So far the governors, the state economic development officials from the three main states (Tennessee, Mississippi, Arkansas) are cooperating. Sustaining their interest and help will be a challenge. Getting the chambers of commerce and the political leaders in these counties and cities to cooperate will also be difficult. The issue is one that stems directly from our traditional ideas of professional success and accomplishment. Those involved as mayors, as economic development officers, as Chamber of Commerce officials, etc., will have to develop deep pride in accomplishments for the region as a whole rather than for their city or county or group. Instead of perceiving success as "what I did for my city," they will have to see success as "what we contributed to the growth of the region."

It is at this nitty-gritty level of personal goals and personal ambitions that the power and possibilities of cooperative ventures break down. In the Mid-South Common Market area there is now a growing group of individuals who are defining the goals, roles and models for sustained cooperative efforts directed toward creation of a world-class community. It is an important experiment that others can learn from—unless, of course, we decide we can still afford to compete against each other and that a win/lose situation is better than a win/win.

Source: Adapted from Jeffrey Hallett, "Cooperation: The Secret to Economic and Social Progress in the 90s." Reprinted by permission of the author. Jeffrey Hallett is principal of The Present Futures Group, Alexandria, Virginia.

cally strong and competitive in the next century. State governments must also assure an adequate revenue base for new regional authorities.

Regional governance should also facilitate more equitable local taxation, and tax-base sharing.

It is especially important to give city and town governments a full partnership role in evolving forms of metropolitan governance. But the purely voluntary or federated forms which regions have adopted in the past fall far short of the shared and focused decision making and accountability regions will need to prosper, and serve their citizens well in the perilous international economy of the 1990s and the next century.

Managing the Demand for Government Services

Norman R. King

The topic of this article is city management and the changing profession. We have two sides of our job. The first is to live and play by the rules (the management side). The second is to help make the rules: help the city council, the state, and the federal government make those rules. This article addresses our role in making the rules. It comes from the conviction that unless we change some of the rules by which we play, we really have no hope to properly manage our cities.

My purposes are twofold: The first is to show a relationship between what I believe are some of the most important economic and moral issues of our time and how they affect the management of cities. The second is to articulate a different perspective about how we must approach the future. I call it *demand management,* as opposed to *supply management.* Basically, the theme that I will be coming back to is that government at all levels is not properly managing the demand for government services, for products and for natural resources; consequently, we are over-consuming them. As a nation, we cannot sustain this level of consumption much longer. My theme is that as managers and as a society, we will have to move from supply management to demand management.

Basic trends

Before talking about the specifics of demand management, I will address four basic trends that are hindering our ability to manage

This article is an edited transcript of a speech delivered at the 42nd Annual Kansas City Management Conference, 26 April 1989, University of Kansas, Lawrence, Kansas. The speech was entitled "Managing the Demand for Government Services: New Direction for City Management."

cities—and, for that matter, our ability to manage this country and this world.

Increasing cost per unit   The first trend is the increasing cost per unit of government services and resources. The law of diminishing returns says that once you scrape off the easiest to get, you spend more money and more energy getting the rest. When we are dealing with resources and many government services we are in a situation of diminishing returns.

The early seventies presented a time in this country, if not in the world, when economics began to reflect the law of diminishing returns. Let me give an example related to the cost of electricity. In the early seventies, for the first time, the cost to produce the extra kilowatt became greater than the average cost that was existing at the time. This was a fundamental difference, because before 1972 or 1973, for the most part, electricity was being produced at a *decreasing* cost per kilowatt. Up to that time, as long as we could assure ourselves that we were actually decreasing the cost of a kilowatt by producing more, it made sense to have a pricing system that encouraged more use: because we replaced more expensive kilowatts with cheaper kilowatts. However, once the cost of the next kilowatt became higher than that of the preceding kilowatt, a new rate structure was needed to give consumers incentives to use less.

We are beginning to get to that point 15 years later. There are some incentives to use less. And what is true for electricity is also true for so many of our basic resources. Fishing is a good example. In spite of a vastly increased capital investment to get more fish, the yield of fish is not increasing worldwide. According to Lester Brown, "Once the growth in human demand reaches the sustainable yield threshold of a given biological system, further increases in demand can be satisfied only by consuming the productive resource base itself, thus causing more rapid shrinkage of the resource."

Not all of this is ecological. Due process (particularly as it has been interpreted by various court decisions around the country in the last 15 years) has also become part and parcel of the law of diminishing returns—to the extent that it simply costs more to hire, fire, or discipline an employee now. There are more hoops to go through to get to the same end product—the goal of which is a tight system of personnel management. I would not argue against the importance of that constitutional provision, but I think that it has gone too far in terms of court interpretations and that it is one of those major factors increasing the cost of government. We do the same thing as we did in the past, but it costs more.

Decreased availability of resources   The second trend is the decrease in funds available to all levels of government except the federal government. We have seen the cuts in federal revenue sharing and the elimination of many federal grants. We are familiar now with the ethic of "enough rather than more" and with the importance of defining what is "necessary" as opposed to what is "good" or "desirable." That's one of the classic questions city councils deal with: determining what is necessary rather than good and desirable. We are in an era of limits, at least at this time, and one of the factors we have to deal with is that there are fewer federal funds to help us out of our financial problems.

Mortgaging the future   The third major trend, and perhaps the most serious, is that we are mortgaging the future. Much of this has to do with the fact that we have passed on costs to future generations in order to maximize present-day consumption.

Some of the ways we have mortgaged the future include the federal budget deficit, unfunded pension systems, pollution of our air and water, and deferred infrastructure maintenance.

Our tax system encourages the wrong things   The fourth basic trend that I would like to set forth is that our tax and pricing systems encourage us to do the wrong things. These "wrong" things concern our tendencies not to save, to over-consume, and to mortgage the future. Many of these incentives are quite unintentional, but we sometimes fail to see how pervasive these incentives are. When I say tax and pricing, I am talking about certain aspects of our taxing system that cause consumers to spend money differently than they might otherwise. And I am talking about deficiencies in our pricing structure that don't fully charge the consumer the total price of using the product. We have created a tax and pricing system which unintentionally gives us incentives to over-consume resources and government services. This is true especially of those government services for which user fees do not apply—such as court systems, fire services, and police services.

One example is housing. The largest single federal housing program we have in this country is assistance to people who own homes and are permitted to write off taxes and mortgage cost for up to two homes. Because of this income tax law, which goes back to the 1940s, when there was not a progressive tax rate, consumers (particularly the more affluent in the higher tax brackets) are "told" that it is better to spend the money on a bigger house than to take a vacation. The point is, incentives in our tax system make owning a house preferable to other kinds of expenditures. That has led to over-consumption of housing in the sense that we have built bigger houses further from our places of work, requiring greater energy expenditures and greater amounts of building materials, than we otherwise would have, because we would have spent this money differently had we not been given this incentive.

Another example is this country's forest policy. The United

States Forest Service operates under a system in which when they sell trees, they not only get a tax credit from the U.S. Treasury, they also get to keep a percentage of the gross sales of the value of the timber sold. If the Forest Service, on the other hand, collects fees for a campground, that money goes to the federal government's general fund. So, what are the incentives to the ranger who wishes to advance in the Forest Service? It's obviously to cut trees. That is probably why we are spending far too much money subsidizing the production and sale of timber on national forest lands than we would be otherwise. In summary, the way we price our government services and resources, including tax policies, is a powerful set of incentives affecting our behavior to do the "wrong" things.

The demand management concept

Now I would like to suggest some solutions, which I have called *demand management*. For all of the above reasons, solving problems by spending more won't work and is no longer possible. We simply must have an alternative. I would suggest that public administration has been very supply oriented. We all had that kind of training: If we have a problem, the solution is to find funds to start a program to solve that problem.

Supply management defines the problem as "not enough of" and the solution as "more of." Demand management offers a different perspective on the same problem. It is a perspective that defines the problem as having too much demand for a service or resource. For public administrators, the solution is to figure out how to manipulate the demand *downward* so we don't have the problem to begin with.

Some examples. One of the big issues that all managers today are dealing with in some way is solid waste disposal. Solid waste is an example of an *exponential* increase in consumption—in this case consumption of close-in land for land-fills. The problem, as we typically would define it in our city halls, is that we don't have enough money to build an incinerator, or a new landfill, or to ship it out of the area. Conversely, the *real* problem is that we have too much waste coming through the system in the first place. That is the demand management perspective. Therefore the solution is to implement a tax and pricing system that reduces the amount of garbage and deals with prevention rather than treatment. That is the essence of demand management. The bottom line is to create incentives, whether they are price, tax or regulation, that create an environment for our citizens, and for you and me, to behave in a manner that reduces the problems we face at the local government level. I would suggest that we really have very few alternatives because of the four basic trends described earlier.

Take the Alaska pipeline as an example. That $5 billion expenditure in the 1970s was unnecessary, considering that we could have spent that same $5 billion on conservation improvements in California at approximately $10,000 per house, and gotten a higher energy return on our investment. The point is, if we had an institutional mechanism to do that, we would still have the oil in Alaska available for when we are really going to need it and we would also be living better now because we would have spent less.

The medical system. The problem is that we have a disease-oriented medical system that places very little emphasis, in terms of individual responsibility and individual incentives, on not getting sick in the first place. The problem is not, as many people believe, one of funding increasing medical care.

So what I am suggesting is a different way of thinking about the role of government. *It is the other side of government.* We don't give up the supply orientation; we still need to operate programs and run them properly. But we need to raise the possibility that perhaps the money should not be spent in the first place; that if we make some changes to reduce the demand for government products and services, we would be better off.

A couple of comments on how conservatives and liberals might view this concept. There is the conservative, who of course likes the emphasis on the free market—the pricing that I have discussed. But that same conservative is probably going to have some trouble with the suggestion that a stronger governmental role is necessary: that is, demand management requires a government that says we are going to price a product at the true cost, including external cost, of using the product. This will cause the market to work correctly, whereas currently the under-costing of many products leads to over-consumption. That is the conservative's problem with what I am proposing: It does require a stronger role for government to allow the market to work properly.

A liberal, on the other hand, doesn't really trust the market system to ration, and will immediately and appropriately ask: "What are we going to do with the poor?" I suggest that we deal with the poor through an income support program, as opposed to looking at every single resource and trying to define an assistance program for food, for energy, for housing, on down the line. As I have already pointed out we frequently do things that are dysfunctional for our society as a whole under the banner of helping the poor.

One example. A Mobil Oil advertisement describing why we shouldn't have higher gas taxes in this country says that "The burden of the hefty hike in gasoline tax would fall most heavily on those least able to pay." What this advertisement doesn't talk about is that about 5% of the total gasoline in this country is consumed by the 20% who are by definition poor. We have policies in this country to keep the price of gasoline artificially low to protect 5% of that consumption, when in fact, 95% of the gasoline is purchased by people who are not poor. Thus, under the banner of protecting the poor, we put some money in our own pockets, because the actual subsidy will be greater for those who use more than for those who use less. To answer the liberals' concern for equity, the only rational approach will be a broadly defined income support system based on total need and not built around subsidizing all the various commodities necessary for life.

The promise of demand management is that it will require less government spending, and we will offer more choices to our citizens in terms of service levels. It will require less regulation, because we are dealing with individual decisions made by thousands of individuals that are more consistent with the aggregate interest of the society. And I would submit that almost any issue we deal with, whether it's parking lots, congestion, pollution, solid waste, trash, drainage, fire service, or medical service, has some relationship to a demand approach. I believe we have the responsibility to constantly ask, "Why do we have the problem in the first place?" And the answer, more often than not, is because of the failure of the pricing system and the tax system to motivate the proper kinds of consumer behavior—which, if done correctly, would make our lives at city hall a lot easier.

Differences between public and private enterprise Let me make just a couple of observations about the differences between public and private enterprise. I think it's crucial because the *effect* of demand for products and services on public versus private corporations is very different. In private business, demand for a product means success. That is how a private enterprise is judged. If more things are sold, a greater profit should result. In government, on the other hand, the demand for services leads to precisely the opposite. Increased demand is not a measure of success. In most cases, it is a measure of the deterioration of the service level.

Libraries are a good example. An outstanding library actually breeds deterioration of service because as the library becomes more popular, more counter space for check-out, more books, and more specialized services are required. This, of course, can only be financed by more general fund money, which puts increased pressure on some other government service or results in a deteriorating level of service. So the first thing to understand about the difference between the public and the private sector is that when you are told, as we all have been: "Private industry cuts back all the time," our response should be: "That's what private industry *should* do, because when they need to cut back, it's a failure of their product to sell. The demand for their product has been reduced. When city hall needs to cut back, it is often because demand for our services has outrun our ability to pay for them. Therefore, we really shouldn't operate like a business but rather should look to how demand for our services can be reduced."

Privatization   The real meaning of privatization is not contracting with private enterprises to supply the certain government services. The real issue is to "privatize" the cost of consuming various resources so that all costs, external and otherwise, are charged to the private user. This alone will reduce the *public* costs of having to treat the consequences of overconsumption (whether that is too much waste, too little freeway space, or too much air pollution).

We have to recognize that there is a constant war going on between the taxpayer and the ratepayer. We are split personalities. We are both at the same time. What we do as a ratepayer/consumer is often dysfunctional to us as a taxpayer.

Our governments are often left to solve problems created by overconsumption because our ratepayer/consumer personality is induced to buy things we shouldn't (or more of something than we otherwise would) because we do not pay the full cost of the product. This leads to the production of additional smog, additional freeway requirements, additional land fills. If we did pay the full cost *privately*, the incidence of those problems as *public* problems of smog, of traffic congestion, and of solid waste would decrease. The most powerful obstacle to better government in this country is the constant and understandable attempt of the private sector to keep their products or services from bearing the true usage cost. The result is that more of the product is consumed than would otherwise be the case, thus forcing the public to try to combat the problem with a more expensive solution. This, in essence, is the struggle between the taxpayer and the consumer.

The reason it is hard to keep abandoned autos off our streets is not management incompetence or even lack of funds. It is a failure of our price system to keep cars from being abandoned. The most significant problem of government is not inefficiency; it is that government must deal with too many unwanted leftovers of privately used goods. Technology actually increases our society's ability to dump these costs on the public. For example, in times past, our primary means of transportation—horses—ate the local hay or grass and left only one public problem; today our automobiles "eat" fuel shipped from Alaska 4,000 miles away. The effects of such consumption have caused great environmental damage along the way (affecting the Alaskan fishing and tourism industries); have caused health problems for thousands; and have caused the deterioration of trees located 100 miles away from the point of consumption. In other words, technology can broaden the negative external impacts of consumption.

It is perhaps the ultimate irony of world politics that as communism is ever more recognized as a failure, the success of capitalism is overpowering the ability of our governments to cope. It is becoming clearer and clearer that neither the theory nor practice of communism has worked: it has not been able to produce enough goods and services that people want and need. But the irony is that communism's demise comes at a time when it also becomes clear that reforms are necessary to ensure that capitalism does not spur so much consumption of finite resources that the survival of our entire world is at stake. We are very close to a Pyrrhic victory over communism.

Role of technology   I would suggest, from a demand management perspective, that technology is one of the greatest motivators of increased government spending. It has increasingly caused us to implement higher standards, which may be good. But higher standards also mean higher costs. The Golden Gate Bridge could not be built today because of higher standards. Kenneth Boulding reminded those of us on the ICMA Future Horizons Committee several years ago that the tombstone of our civilization will say "Killed by high standards."

The issue of health care costs provides another example. The percentage of GNP spent on health care has gone from 6-7% in 1970 to 12% in 1988. Are we really getting a return for the increased spending? The answer is generally no. We have extended life a little longer, but in terms of birth, death and longevity, we are comparable to other industrial nations, except for the fact that we spend, in some cases, double the amount of our GNP on health care.

I am questioning the whole emphasis on medical technology: are we spending money on the wrong thing? One example is Cesarean rates. In 1965, 4.5% of births were Cesarean; in 1986, 25% were Cesarean. There has been no change in death rates. The reason for the increase has to do with incentives in the system, primarily malpractice insurance. This is another example of spending a lot more ($5,000 instead of $3,000) for something that doesn't have a productive effect on our society.

Technology is increasingly dictating our spending priorities. We are not making conscious decisions about who and what to assist. We delude ourselves that high health costs can be controlled by better management. But the real issue has nothing to do with better management: it's basically an ethical problem, a matter of deciding where we are going to use our technology, medical or otherwise.

Yet another problem is that the decisions for allocating the rationing of technology are often being made through the court system. For instance, liability awards are becoming social welfare expenditures allocated by court decisions. The administrative costs of court-awarded welfare expenditures are very high—often 30-60%

for attorney's fees alone, excluding court costs. If a welfare program in any city or county had an administration fee of 30-60% for handing out welfare checks, the city or county manager wouldn't be around very long. But we tolerate a system that rations our technology through liability and malpractice awards with 30-60% administrative costs. In any case, technology has forced us into a defensive position of overdoing, over-designing, over-prescribing, over-operating, etc., all in order to protect ourselves from potential liability.

Application of demand management

Let me now suggest a few ways in which we can begin to implement demand management in city hall.

Health insurance   One way to implement demand management is to look at our own medical insurance system. What signals do we give to our employees to use or overuse medical insurance? In my own case a few years ago we faced a 60% increase in medical premiums. We got that down to only a 20% increase, by working with our insurance firm to institute some incentives which focused on individual responsibility, like a wellness program. There are still some cities that actually provide 100% of the cost of family medical insurance. What does that lead to? It leads to the employee not even thinking about the fact that medical care costs money. Whereas some co-payment, even if it is just 10%, motivates a different employee attitude.

Transportation policy   One of the big issues in California is the construction of new roads and freeways to handle increasing automobile use. There are several ways to finance the construction. One is for voters to approve a sales tax increase. This is what occurred in Riverside County. It is a bad policy because the sales tax totally disassociates the tax payer from the rate payer, the user from the producer of the revenue. The non-driver subsidizes the driver, the cost of driving appears lower than it really is, and non-auto transit appears less desirable. At least a gasoline tax begins to place the cost of freeway expansion on the car user. A toll road is by far the most efficient way of allocating the cost of the use of the roadway to the user.

The point is, when a non-use tax like a sales tax or a general tax is used to build a new freeway, we squander the power that a demand-depressing user fee could bring to bear. We give up the ability to raise money for a specific purpose, and we give up the ability to reduce the use. If we charge people the true cost of commuting, we can depress freeway demand, render other transportation alternatives relatively more economical, and reduce the subsidy from the non-user to many more affluent users.

User fees In general, the rule should be: Don't use taxes (which have no behavioral effects) when you can institute fees. Specifically, this means imposing user fees for services whose consumers can be readily identified and therefore held accountable for the cost of consumption. Remember that the taxpayer pays *without* reference to use, and the ratepayer pays *with* reference to use. To give an example, though not an exemplary one: Water services in Palm Springs are provided by a special district governed by five locally elected board members. About one-half the cost of water we consume in Palm Springs is reflected on the tax bill, and the other half is collected in the monthly service charges. This, of course, violates the basic premise that whenever the user can be identified, the whole cost of the product should be allocated to the consumer. Water conservation in our desert community is important, and it has been suggested that it would be very simple to encourage residents to reduce consumption by allocating the full cost of consumption to the monthly service fee and eliminating the revenues supporting the water system from the property tax. Unfortunately, the members of the water board do not seem to believe in the relationship between price and demand when applied to water consumption.

The irony is that as capitalists, we believe that the laws of supply and demand work well in the private sector—but we disbelieve their validity in the public sector. This is in spite of the fact that properly implemented pricing systems will promote the conservation of many government resources. Again, user fees are not just a way to raise money. They are also a way to improve the efficiency of allocating resources, thus affirming the rationing function of price.

Criminal justice There are a number of opportunities in this area. For example, false alarm ordinances that penalize those whose alarm systems are operating improperly reduce service requirements of the police department. In Palm Springs, false alarms fell 30% after such an ordinance was imposed.

An Arizona law allows persons convicted of certain drug charges to be assessed the cost of the government investigation. California now has a law under which up to $500 can be assessed to reimburse the local police department for its expenses in handling a traffic accident in which alcohol is involved and the offender was legally drunk.

We had the following situation in Palm Springs. A grand theft a couple of years ago cost our city $15,000 in overtime alone. The owner got all his property back (one million bucks worth). The judge's sentence was 200 hours of public service for the offense. I don't care if we coddle criminals; I don't care if we rehabilitate them; I don't care if we punish them. But why should we subsidize them? It doesn't make any sense: 200 public service hours as payment to society for having to spend more than $15,000 to catch the thief in the first place, to say nothing of jury time, court costs, and so on.

Waste pricing As a rule our society fails to price accurately the cost of disposing of used products. This results in increased solid waste, increased toxic waste, and increased air pollution. The basic proposition is that pollution is an uncaptured resource. The trick is to implement a regulatory and pricing system that captures resources using the fewest dollars *before* they cause a burden to society.

When disposal costs are not included in the price of a product, several negative effects occur: larger governmental expenditures are necessary to handle the problem at the treatment stage (such as a land-fill solution); the cost of treatment is generally greater than the cost of prevention; less recycling occurs; greater negative side effects are inflicted on the population; and the role of government ultimately increases, as more regulations are imposed telling people how to do things (as opposed to having price incentives consistent with the goals of society).

The solution, affluent fees, puts a price on the side effects of using a product. It also makes it more attractive not to discard the product and not to use it in a way that has negative effects on society. As Edwin Mills has stated, "Economic incentives are the only viable option. The main reason for illegal disposal is that it is cheaper than compliance with the law and it is in the public interest to reverse the order of these costs."

The bottle bills imposed in many states are the simplest example of an economic incentive that discourages pollution and creates a market that encourages recycling of such materials. These laws have unleashed thousands of "roadside" police. The same principle in more sophisticated forms can be imposed on products ranging from automobiles (to discourage abandoned automobiles) to toxic waste.

Marvin Katzman supports this view. The guiding philosophy is that the cost of materials to manufacturers should reflect the downstream cost of disposal or detoxification. If a material is economically recyclable, then downstream cost may be negligible. Of the two alternative materials which cost the same to produce, the one that is recyclable is cheaper than the one that must be discarded.

Flood control Flood control and drainage control is a major problem facing many communities. Many cities are implementing innovative water retention incentives for new development. Credit is given for on-site retention of water through various ponding mechanisms, thus reducing the amount the developer would pay in drainage fees which finance the off-site drainage system. Savings to the community is reflected in the downsizing of the size of the drainage system necessary to protect the community.

The fire service   The emphasis on built-in protection (e.g., sprinkler systems) is an important application of demand management to the fire service. In addition, many communities are bolstering prevention and inspection efforts. A few communities are beginning to experiment with municipal fire insurance to provide incentives for the improvement of local fire prevention measures. For instance, the City of Visalia, California, concluded in 1985 that its citizens paid about $6.0 million a year in fire insurance and about $1.3 million a year for its fire department (through taxes). However, the community's average fire loss over the past ten years had been only $300,000 per year. The city questioned whether the performance of Visalia's fire prevention system had been given adequate credit by the insurance companies.

Tax policy   It will come as no surprise that I would advocate some kind of increase in taxes on consumption, such as the value-added tax. This tax might well exempt a base amount of consumption and expenditures in order to protect the less affluent. It should be noted that Western Europe, in particular, has higher private savings rates probably because the European tax system relies heavily on value-added taxes.

Another change in our tax policy that I would recommend is drastic restrictions on open-ended government entitlements. Most entitlements do not go to the poor. Non-means-tested entitlements account for 38% of the federal budget. Only 20% of this amount goes to the poor. Only 8% of the federal budget goes to support means-tested entitlements, and less than 15% of total federal spending goes to the poor. If we are to make a dent in the federal budget deficit, we must successfully move toward means-tested entitlements and the end of entitlements for those who do not meet such tests.

Welfare and income policy   It will come as no surprise that I would also advocate some sort of income support program to those in need. Only in this manner can our society assist the poor without encouraging over-consumption by everyone. The basic problem of our present welfare system is the failure to distinguish between *circumstance* and *need*. Thus, many of our welfare benefits go to persons of a certain age as opposed to persons of a certain age who are in need.

I would argue for some sort of welfare policy that provides basic income support and is not based on the piecemeal approach of food stamps, energy stamps, housing stamps, etc., to solve the problems of the poor.

Conclusion

I have tried to outline some basic changes affecting our profession and present a perspective on what I have called demand management. It may take awhile for ICMA to develop management seminars or to issue its first demand management Green Book, but I believe that as professionals we must move in this direction. Unless the rules of the game change, it will be increasingly difficult for us to help our local communities survive in the next century. I believe that demand management provides an opportunity to make our jobs easier and cities more livable.

The Future of Council-Manager Government

—————————————— Chester A. Newland

In 1978 the International City Management Association (ICMA) Committee on Future Horizons launched a two-year examination of prospects for the profession of local government management in the year 2000. That Committee studied society generally and local government in particular to gain useful insights. In an initial publication in 1979, the Committee reported cautiously optimistic conclusions looking toward "new worlds of service."[1] The focus of the anticipated service challenge identified by the Committee was highlighted a year later in the ICMA book *The Essential Community: Local Government in the Year 2000.* That focus was on the neighborhood level, where, the Committee said, "everything comes together."[2]

That optimistic focus and other major conclusions of the ICMA study of a decade ago provide useful points of departure to assess prospects for council-manager government in the year 2000. Added experience of the past ten years and the shorter span of time to the turn of the century make the present effort considerably less ambitious than that of the Horizons Committee.

This present assessment, like the earlier ICMA project, examines past and current developments as bases for thinking about and creating the future. It accepts the Horizon Committee's premise that the future is in part conditional; it can be created to some extent by deliberate actions, and it should be. In short, the chief purpose of futures studies is not simply to project what may be but to provide bases for actions to bring about more desired future circumstances.

Reprinted with permission from H. George Frederickson, ed., *Ideal and Practice in Council-Manager Government* (Washington, D.C.: ICMA, 1989). © 1989, ICMA.

This analysis consists of three parts. Initially, work of the Future Horizons Committee is summarized and briefly placed in two contexts: first, that of the longer history of council-manager government and, then, that of futures disciplines practiced by professional local government managers. In the second part, structural issues of council-manager government are highlighted first and then roles of the council, manager, mayor, and other key officials are discussed. Many of these old and current concerns were passed over lightly by the Horizons Committee, but their significance was recognized then, and their importance has grown during the past decade. In the concluding part, the environment of local government in the United States is briefly assessed in terms of future prospects. Such assessment constituted much of the work of the Committee in 1978–1980, and some of its projections were impressively on target—while subsequent developments have proved other conclusions wrong or irrelevant.

Kenneth Boulding cautioned ICMA conferees in 1979 that futures studies are the most celestial of celestial sciences. It is like looking into a cloudy crystal ball. Some clouds of the 1970s have dissipated over the years; other old ones are closer; some large, dark, unpredicted clouds have moved over the horizon, and sometimes they almost seem to dominate today's scene. Bases for much optimism about professionally managed local government are now present, however, as many were a decade ago. As then, some of the most sustaining grounds for hope for the future stem from idealism which has deep roots in American culture. The Committee in 1979 quoted Richard Childs's 1918 advice: "The great city managers of tomorrow will be those who push beyond the old horizons and discover new worlds of service." [3]

That ideal of public service and its twin discipline of democracy—civic duty—are fundamental to the dynamic balance of council-manager government. Purposes and processes of constitutional government must also be sustained in the larger environment of American society, or that delicate balance is unlikely to survive at the local level. That is much of the challenge as the United States moves toward the year 2000. That challenge, most evident in the widespread growth of transactional politics and the decline of transformational politics, is even more evident today than it was in the exchange environment of government that became dominant nationally by the 1970s.

Past experience and futures disciplines

Experience with council-manager government during its first three-quarters of a century is briefly defined here in terms of four successive periods, three with relatively clear contours plus the current period, in which diversity makes definition difficult. Conclusions and disciplines of professional urban managers as futurists, particularly as highlighted by ICMA's Horizons Committee, are then discussed.

Past clarity, growing diversity   For purposes of "futures assessment," the three most easily defined past periods of council-manager history are these: the Political Reform Period, from the early Progressive Era into the 1940s, the Structural Discipline Period, from the late 1940s into the 1960s, and the Social Activism Period, from the 1960s through the 1970s.

The Political Reform Period which gave birth to council-manager government was, to a significant extent, a time of transformational politics. From the years of the nation's Constitutional Centennial to the Sesquicentennial, reformers used politics to attack spoils, inefficiencies, and related governmental problems. The Centennial gave occasion for many to reflect on how the United States, born out of the transformational idealism of the closing years of the Enlightenment, had shifted course since the 1820s. American governments had become objects and instruments of a market-type exchange for private gain. Opposition to that corruption and dismay over the loss of American idealism ushered in a new period in which transformational politics sometimes prevailed again, as in the incremental creation of council-manager government nearly halfway through the larger Reform Era.

In terms of problems of the 1970s and 1980s and projections through the 1990s, it is worth reiterating that council-manager government and related reforms were not initially attempts to escape from politics. Reform was aimed at displacing the corruption of transactional politics with the idealism of transformational politics. Council-manager government in its early decades was designed as a *political* means to facilitate a civic culture of integrity and informed accomplishment.

The Structural Discipline Period which lasted from sometime after World War Two into the early 1960s came to be dominated by public administration orthodoxy. Two doctrines prevailed: executive aggrandizement and the politics-administration dichotomy. The latter doctrine *in that period* can be described as one of attempted escape from politics generally. But in terms of issues of the last two decades of the twentieth century, it is principally the public administration doctrine of the powerful executive that drastically altered perceptions of council-manager government during the 1940s, 1950s, and 1960s, generating later pressures for political reform of what some had come to see as a detached or neutral form of government. During earlier years of its creation, this form was routinely known as *council*-manager government, and it was perceived as a *political* reform plan—anything but detached or neutral. By the 1950s, it was often referred to in public administration circles as the *city man-*

ager form. Engineers who had earlier reported as subordinate managers to politically superior councils were increasingly displaced by students of public administration who had been taught to value executive power and to have disdain for politics and politicians. Structures of executive power became inviolate in "The Plan." The manager's budget became a bastion of executive power, barely subject to council modification. The manager came to have a near monopoly on information, subject chiefly to inquiry only by the council as a whole. Councilmember contacts with operating officials other than the manager became virtually impossible, often illegal. Appointed managers prospered in power, but the old politics of reform gradually withered, and by the late 1960s that greatly expanded executive power often lacked the authority of popular support. The structural disciplines of "The Plan" undermined councils as vehicles of authoritative government, threatening the future viability of this governmental form.

The Social Activism Period that erupted during the 1960s challenged both professionally managed and politically dominated governments. Some professional managers, schooled in what later came to be called New Public Administration thinking, responded vigorously with proposals of "new worlds of service." Keith Mulrooney, then City Manager of Claremont, California, for example, along with others, filled a symposium in *Public Administration Review* with challenges for managers to provide needed policy leadership to deal with urgent social conflicts and needs.[4] That orientation remained one of managerial dominance, consistent with experience of the Structural Discipline Period, but it resulted in newly visible managerial involvement in issues of nonconsensus politics. Conflicts characterized many issues of the 1960s, leading to a period of political dissensus in America that persists to today.[5] By the late 1970s, this new political environment led to a period of concerns among professional managers, civic leaders, and others about the future of professionally managed local government. These concerns, leavened with positive idealism, resulted in formation of the Future Horizons Committee, appointed in 1978 by ICMA President Bob Kipp, City Manager of Kansas City, with George Schrader, City Manager of Dallas, as the committee chair. That development acknowledged what informed professionals in local government had long understood: council-manager governments were functioning under increasingly diverse forms and varied processes in efforts to satisfy changing definitions of effectiveness while subject to new pressures for economy and efficiency. It was time to search the horizons for new directions.

Diversity and futures disciplines   Diversity characterized professionally managed local governments by 1978. Orthodoxy of "The Plan" was not simply challenged but already significantly eroded:

election of at-large councilmembers was increasingly displaced by single-member districts; council staffs were being created and expanded; mayors were exercising strong leadership—even dominating some governments—while relying on professional managers as deputies; some managers were employed under contracts with severance provisions; hierarchical control over information and some operations had been reduced; and forms of popular participation had greatly expanded. The mayor-council form of government also continued to be popular in both the biggest cities and smallest towns. Those developments were scarcely touched upon by the Future Horizons Committee. They were continuing issues from the past, and ICMA had dealt with them to some extent a decade earlier. New goals had been established in 1969; the International City Managers Association had become the International City Management Association; and the chief organization issue that occupied ICMA by 1978 was whether another name change should be considered, substituting "local" or "urban" for "city" management.

Orthodoxy had ceased to be the discipline of many professional local managers. "Futures studies" filled the gap for some. For ICMA, the Horizons Committee recommended disciplines of lifelong learning and professional action as crucial:

Study of the known and the unknown—to attain a mature balance of confidence and humility in the face of changes.

Awareness of situations and diversity—to appreciate both the positive science of "One Best Way" and the open inquiry of contingency management.

Practice of values and processes of constitutional democracy—to facilitate popular self-governance and a rule of law.

As noted earlier, the Horizons Committee stressed the conditional character of history: that probable and possible futures can be changed. As practical futurists, in short, professional managers can make a difference. The Horizons Committee concluded that the chief responsibility of professionally expert managers as futurists is to facilitate a continuing search for reasonableness in public affairs—to facilitate constitutionally based self-governance, firmly grounded in values of transformational politics, human dignity, and a rule of law.

Also recommended by the Committee were practical strategies to contend with expected conditions of the 1980s. Five were stressed in 1979, and the assumptions about the future upon which they were based turned out to be largely accurate: "Learn to get by modestly, regulate the demand for local government services, be skeptical of federal dollars and the dependencies they cause, emphasize decentralization over regionalization of services, look at new services needed as a result of the [changing] population."[6] In short, while the

Horizons Committee projected a future in which managers would need to "be even more idealistic," much of the focus was on realism about future challenges.

Structural issues

Twenty years after ICMA's self-examination in light of structural issues and related changes in council-manager government and ten years after the Future Horizons Committee, developments among professionally managed local government have resulted in sustained concerns about structures of urban government. Projections into the future require assessment of these concerns and the structural issues behind them. This assessment first deals briefly with conflicting doctrines and dynamics with respect to roles of the council, the manager, the mayor, and other officers. The treatment sketches issues about roles in practical terms of both charter provisions and changing urban dynamics. This part concludes with a summary of these issues in terms of three sets of contrasts between the council-manager and mayor-council forms.

The council: Control of purposes and resources   General agreement prevails that the council in professionally managed government has ultimate authority over purposes and resources. Beyond that, many differences exist about councils. Three sets of practical issues of varied scope that seem certain to persist into the future are noted here.

Elections: At-large, district, partisan?   Most important in terms of "The Plan" are two issues: (1) council election at large or by district and (2) nonpartisan or partisan political elections.

The first issue has often been driven in recent years by court orders to elect councilmembers from single-member districts to facilitate minority electoral power. Clearly, district election enhances "neighborhood" power. "The Plan" rejected districts for precisely that reason, favoring a "community-at-large" orientation. Generally, such at-large elections result in selection of councilmembers with higher educational and occupational status; also they are usually Anglos.

Media and electoral dynamics may be redefining the nature of the at-large/district controversy. Communitywide media coverage —particularly cable television and local commercial television news—may be an effective force to heighten shared awareness of some public matters. However, expanded media influence and national political dynamics have resulted in escalating costs of many local elections. At-large campaigns commonly cost much more than in districts, making them more subject to special-interest financing; district elections, in turn, may become relatively invisible, making them victims of special-interest manipulation.

One result of these pressures has been heightened, conflict-oriented politics whether communitywide or neighborhood issues are involved. That is a nationwide political phenomenon; television, a medium that plays communitywide or—even more often—nationwide, has become a force of dissensus by focusing on 15- to 90-second bites of mostly conflict-oriented or sensational events. Local news reports focus vastly more time on homicides and auto accidents, barroom brawls, and political shenanigans than on matters of broader or deeper character. Accompanying these developments, partisanship has been on the rise in council elections, although many jurisdictions formally continue nonpartisan forms even when high partisanship informally dominates. The trend toward partisanship is linked to national trends like those noted above, and it seems destined to continue at least into the near future.

Other pressures that account for heightened politics include these: Consensus about roles of government has declined. Party competition has spread nationally, greatly reducing regions of one-party politics, as in the former "solid South" and the Republican Midwest and New England. High costs of media politics have forced renewed dependence on some party apparatus for financing elections, with renewed linkages through computerized donor lists from precincts through city, state, and national levels. Special interests have increasingly formed parallel networks that reach from precincts to the national level. Individuals who aspire to offices beyond local government again see council election as a springboard to "higher office." All of these developments are linked to a general trend from the late 1960s through the 1980s toward partisan politicization and deinstitutionalization.

Council size, terms, and compensation   These three issues are interrelated in practice. "The Plan" favored small, unremunerated councils. Members generally served limited terms.

Recent trends favor slightly larger numbers, particularly following population increases, although tendencies have not been to create councils as large as those in strong-mayor cities of comparable size. No signs suggest much change from modest growth in council size in the near future.

Before the shift to district elections and heightened partisanship, terms of councilmembers under "The Plan" tended to be voluntarily self-limiting, usually to two short terms of two to four years. Also, compensation of councilmembers was rare under "The Plan," and they often paid their own expenses incurred in public service. Time devoted to council responsibilities was commonly limited to a few hours a week; the manager and other employees were expected to perform all full-time work. Except in smaller communities, these earlier practices have changed. Councilmembers in larger cities are now commonly compensated, and most expect expenses to be reimbursed. In larger governments, compensation often approaches levels that encourage some individuals to value it as a desirable, full-time income or as a substantial addition to other resources. Provision of insurance, retirement benefits, and such perquisites as automobiles and telephones is no longer rare.

Continuation in office beyond one or two short terms has increased where partisanship, compensation, and perquisites have expanded. While questions have arisen in recent years about imposing limits in the charter on the maximum number of terms councilmembers may serve, the new Model Charter of the National Civic League does not provide for such limits, and such limits appear to be unlikely in the future. Terms of mayors are a related issue that will be discussed later.

Council staff and committees   Council-manager government initially contemplated that the entire administrative apparatus would serve, through the manager, as "staff" to the council, a practice that generally continued even in larger cities until the 1970s. The original idea was one variation of the reform movement: election on a short ballot of a visible few who would constitute a government of unity, not one characterized by separation of powers. In the absence of such separation, council staff was not required. However, during the Structural Discipline Period, councils increasingly found themselves fenced off from the administrative apparatus of government, shunted into obscurity by the growing public administration orthodoxy of the powerful executive. Also, professional managers often came to dominate policy initiatives. When the Social Activism Period followed, council workloads increased, councilmembers often found themselves hard pressed to fulfill constituents' demands, and pressures grew to provide staff assistance to councilmembers.

Staffs developed along two directions in the 1970s and 1980s: (1) liaison staff to serve the council as a whole and (2) staff to individual councilmembers. Liaison staff, in turn, commonly took two forms: (1) under control of the manager and (2) under the control of the mayor and other councilmembers. Individual council staff also developed in two directions: (1) secretarial and other office staff, commonly nonpartisan careerists, and (2) district and policy staff, often exempt from civil service and commonly partisan. Today, councilmembers in larger jurisdictions often utilize both sorts of staff, and the council as a whole may also rely on some common "legislative affairs" organization.

As councils have expanded in size and as workloads have grown, some have taken on additional trappings of legislatures, most notably committee forms of organization. These committees have sometimes employed staffs that function as budgetary and functional policy analysts.

As a result of the development of specialized council staff—a legislative apparatus—council-manager government in a few cases has come to resemble a system of separation of powers. Following the Future Horizons project, some members of the Future Horizons Committee started reemphasizing the value of unity of authority in the council, as in a parliamentary system, with the manager and other top administrators responsible for providing direct staff assistance to councilmembers. These alternative ways of approaching council-manager relations—separation of powers versus unity of authority—seem certain to continue at the forefront of future controversy over forms of local government.

However, automated information systems and related high-tech capacities are reshaping council-manager relations. One contradiction between the old orthodoxy of the Structural Discipline Period and the realities of new information technology illustrates the dramatic change that is underway. The old doctrine was that the manager was the single channel of communication between the council and the administrative apparatus. Today, council offices are sometimes linked by computers to information systems that provide relatively real-time information on tax rolls, budget status, physical planning projects, and varied policy agendas. Increasingly, such information and much more is available at computer workstations to administrative and council staff at most levels. Sometimes, citizens can also access such information through personal phone lines or at public-access computer stations at municipal or county facilities. This new openness of information facilitates some renewed unity or "community" in council-manager government. It has already altered the environment of council-manager relations dramatically, and that trend will continue.

The manager: Control of expertise and implementation
While high technology is increasingly eroding the barriers to information flow from the administrative apparatus to the council (and sometimes in the reverse direction), managers still control most of the administrative expertise and methods of implementing council policies. Some exceptions to that arrangement have been common since the early days of "The Plan," however, and others have increased in importance.

Old exceptions, new forms   Civil service employees and planners are two relatively old exceptions to nearly exclusive managerial control of administration. These were exceptions because of the special value placed on them during the Political Reform Period.

Civil service commissions were commonly created to exercise control of personnel operations in the early decades of the council-manager plan. They sometimes controlled all personnel, including recruitment and examination of key administrators. In other cases, at a minimum, they commonly provided oversight of police and fire personnel functions. That old structure has been significantly altered in many governments since the 1960s. Personnel operations have been transferred increasingly to control of managers, and functions of civil service commissions have eroded, except for continuation of appellate oversight for selected employee groups. Expansion of collective bargaining has been the chief cause of the change; bilateralism requires a "management" party not only at the bargaining table but in the day-to-day implementation of labor-management agreements. This development appears likely to continue into the foreseeable future. While unionization and collective bargaining have declined in the private sector, they remain vigorous in the increasingly political environment of government.

While managers have gained enlarged authority over personnel operations vis-à-vis civil service commissions, collective bargaining has resulted in pressures in support of enlarged council intrusions into labor-management relations. While collective bargaining orthodoxy is against such council involvement, except possibly for ratification of final contract provisions, political realities often bring union leaders into direct relationships with councilmembers. Police and firefighters are commonly involved in highly visible electoral campaigns, and other employee unions often engage in similar politics. *Quid pro quos* are expected in labor-management relations, and they are often paid. With the escalation of partisanship—and of the costs of council elections—this new form of the old "civil service exception" to managerial control is likely to continue.

Physical planning and land use constitute the other old exception. Planning never moved far in the direction of managerial dominance, but it has changed in ways that are likely to continue into the future. The old reform ideal was linked to the garden-city movement and thus to the value of high citizen involvement in planning and beautification; but it was also realistic in efforts to insulate physical planning and zoning from corrupting influences of land speculators, railroads, and other special interests. Thus, "insulated" citizen planning boards were created, and professional planners commonly reported both to them and to the manager—in addition to attending many or most council meetings. As land speculators became "homogenized" as developers during the years following World War Two, planning operations came increasingly under their influence. By the 1970s, development and developers again became important sources of political finances, and councils became more directly involved in planning and land use. By the 1980s, such council involvement became common. During the years these changes occurred, professional planners turned increasingly to managerial leadership in efforts to maintain reasonable levels of expertise and integrity in planning operations. Thus, new forms of both managerial control and exceptions to it have developed, and these complex council-manager-planner-citizen-developer relationships will continue.

New exceptions, varied forms   Police review boards constitute a new exception to managerial control over administration. Some other citizen-control and involvement mechanisms that developed in the 1960s and 1970s also remain important and controversial.

Many larger cities have created police review boards in response to political action by minority groups alleging police brutality. Law enforcement personnel have almost always opposed such boards. In council-manager cities, this controversy has a special twist to it. If the police department is under the direction of the manager like other administrative units, should a review board be appointed by and/or report to (or advise) the manager, the police chief—or the council? Often, exceptions to managerial control existed prior to emergence of the police review board issue in appointments of police and/or fire chiefs. Councils have sometimes made these appointments directly; more often the manager has made them, sometimes subject to council consent. Local situations determine how these decisions are made, and general future trends are not discernible. Where professionally oriented or employee-controlled safety services are desired, insulation from citizen oversight is workable; where politically responsive services are preferred, enhanced "popular" control is workable. In either case, because of the escalating importance of partisan politics and the political power of police and fire unions in local elections, extensive employee control over public safety operations is likely to continue.

Varied forms of citizen-involvement mechanisms were developed during the "Great Society" years and later as a result of New Public Administration thinking. Those developments of "civism," their rise, and their partial decline during the Reagan years, are too well known for review here. One feature of these mechanisms distinguishes many of them from citizen-involvement practices of the Political Reform Period, and that difference is vital in contemplation of the future of council-manager government. The old citizen involvement was outside the arena of administration. The "New Civism" of the 1960s injected citizens into administrative processes, as in neighborhood advisory councils to comment on implementation of physical plans and zoning policies or as in increased use of volunteers in law enforcement, recreation programs, and public education. The Future Horizons Committee generally favored such citizen involvement and urged professional managers to facilitate these and other mechanisms of self-governance—but with disciplined means to reduce chances of their takeover or manipulation by special interests with objectives contrary to those of "The Essential

Community." Despite this injunction of a decade ago, retrenchment pressure and other national political pressures resulted in reduced attention to citizen-involvement mechanisms in the 1980s. Those cutback pressures continue to be powerful and are likely to characterize the future.

Accountability: Changed technology, shared information The executive budget had become a fixed tenet of public administration orthodoxy by the Structural Discipline Period. An annual external audit, under the control of the council, became an expected accountability tool. Public financial operations in larger jurisdictions have multiplied in complexity in recent decades, requiring internal controls that facilitate unbroken tracking of all receipts and expenditures. Automated internal financial controls routinely perform these functions today, making it possible to track expenditures from initial authorizations through preaudited approvals of spending, delivery, payments, internal post audits, and periodic external audits.

Typically, the council-manager charter still provides that the council is completely responsible for the external audit function. But with respect to internal financial controls, the comptroller function is essentially an administrative responsibility of the manager. Neither function can be independent of the other, however, and today automated systems facilitate widely shared information among councilmembers and their staffs, managerial officials, line administrators, external auditors, and possibly others, including interested citizens. This may result in new forms of council "intrusions" into administrative processes; the old rule that councilmembers are to deal with the administrative apparatus only through the manager is out of date when computer terminals in council offices can be routinely used to probe for information—without personal contacts with subordinate administrators. Managerial flexibility may be significantly limited. These present realities of council-manager government will continue in importance into the future.

The mayor: Visible brokerage and focus The most obvious challenge to the future of council-manager government has been in the means of selection and the roles of the mayor. These changes have resulted from the growing partisan politicization of local government since the start of the Social Activism Period. Changes that have strengthened the mayors in many council-manager governments are likely to continue in the future because they have facilitated visible brokerage and focus. Although even more drastic changes—adoption of mayor-council government or mayor/manager-council government—will continue to be proposed, the deficiencies of mayor-dominant systems may continue to defeat such drastic changes, particularly in an era of economic stringency and public-sector complexity.

Changes within the council-manager plan   Authority of mayors has been strengthened in varied ways to provide "political leadership" within council-manager government. Three changes have been common and are likely to continue into the future, at least in larger governments.

Changes in the selection of mayors have taken a variety of forms. "The Plan" provided for selection by councilmembers from among themselves, and the office was sometimes rotated. Direct, at-large popular election is not unusual now. Governments which adopt district election of councilmembers and at-large election of the mayor greatly enlarge the relative authority of the mayor. The mayoral election may or may not be synchronous with council election. With direct election of the mayor, the level of partisan politics escalates, and politicians are more attracted to the office as a stepping stone toward other political offices. Costs of elections increase, with resulting changes in the influence of contributors.

The mayor in council-manager government may exercise authority over the council agenda and in appointments to boards and other nonadministrative positions. Traditionally, professional managers formulated agendas in consultation with the mayor or council, and most still do. Even then, without dominating formulation of the agenda, a mayor typically manages the council agenda during meetings. A council which is organized with the trappings of a legislature, however, may have a rules committee to control the agenda, although the rules committee can be an instrument of enhanced mayoral power only if the mayor controls appointment of council committees. Bureaucratization of councils—with expanded use of council committees and legislative staff offices—was a tendency in large cities following politicization in the 1960s and 1970s, and it was typically designed to strengthen the mayor. Rules and finance committees may be chaired by the mayor in such arrangements. A central legislative services office may also be controlled by the mayor. Such developments detract from the fundamental character of council-manager government—undivided, community-oriented authority in the council as a whole—and inject elements of separation of powers into the local government. While bureaucratization was the tendency into the early 1980s, no trend into the 1990s is discernible.

Appointment by the mayor of citizen boards and nonadministrative commissions and officials is a common source of enhanced power. Advice and consent of the council to such appointments remains the rule, however, and that pattern will likely continue.

Mayor-dominant forms   Mayor-council government and other mayor-dominant forms have demonstrated weaknesses when compared to council-manager government, and those are likely to continue into the future, generating support for professionally managed government. Three chief contrasts are these:

1. Mayor-dominant forms are more conflict prone, with increased partisanship and special-interest brokerage.
2. Governmental workforces and expenditures are typically larger, proportionately, in mayor-dominant governments.
3. Departmental actions tend to be quasi-autonomous, with reduced coordination and collaboration, in strong-mayor systems.

Other officials: Situational differences Despite its short-ballot origins, council-manager government has generally functioned with some elected or appointed officials who are independent of the manager, especially in county governments. The attorney is commonly independent, and managers often find that troublesome— particularly when an "abominable no man" fills that office. The clerk generally has a community power base and distinctive responsibilities. Police chiefs may be independent of the manager, and sheriffs are almost always elected. Judges are virtually all independent. No trends are discernible with respect to such "deviations" within council-manager governments. Situational variables will continue to determine them.

Structural alternatives: 1990s precursors? Diversity characterized council-manager governments at the time of the Future Horizons Committee, and variations have continued to increase. Nonetheless, it remains possible to contrast council-manager and mayor-council governments in terms of three sets of ideal characteristics which will continue to be important in the future. All of these were illustrated in the preceding discussion:

1. Council-manager government facilitates more collaborative civic authority, combined with coordinated, institutionalized administration. Mayor-council government encourages separation of powers with the focus on mayoral leadership, but administration is more fragmented and *ad hoc.*
2. Transformational politics with a collaborative, community-wide orientation is the ideal of the council-manager form. Transactional politics facilitating brokerage among differing interests is the ideal of the mayor-council form.
3. Professionally expert administration is the ideal in council-manager government, with neutrally equal access and responsiveness. Politically sensitive administration is the ideal in the mayor-council form, with nonroutinization to facilitate responsiveness.

The positive values associated with mayor-council government have been increasingly incorporated into council-manager forms. Orthodoxy of "The Plan" has eroded, and diversity now prevails. The ideals of council-manager government persist as fundamental. However, changes in the environment of local government will continue to challenge those ideals in the future. Those changes and challenges are the concluding subject here.

Changes and future challenges

Corresponding to developments considered by the Future Horizons Committee, at least six categories of environmental change will impact the future of council-manager government: (1) economic, (2) natural resource, (3) demographic, (4) social, (5) science and technology, and (6) political and governmental.[7] The first five are only briefly sketched here as one set of factors to impact the future, and then relevant political conditions are summarized.

Broad horizons   Economic interdependence worldwide will continue indefinitely, and the United States' peculiar position as the world's largest debtor nation will persist into the foreseeable future.

Water, air, and energy resources—and possibly weather patterns—will continue to be threatened. Environmental protection costs will rise, or resources will be seriously impaired.

The older population, which grew at twice the rate of other age groups during the 1970s–1980s, will continue to increase disproportionately.[8] Females, whose life expectancy averages over seven years longer than that of males, will continue to outlive men, although the gap will narrow slightly. Anglos will constitute less than two-thirds of the population by the year 2000. Hispanic and Black females are younger, with the highest projected birthrates.

Only 15 percent of new entrants into the workforce will be Anglo males during the years to the turn of the century. With 62 percent of all working-age women in the workforce in 1988, females will continue to expand their share of jobs. Retirement age may cease to decline or level off and then begin to rise during the next decade, reversing a downward trend in which nearly two-thirds of workers in the mid-1980s retired before age 65, over half by 62. Changes in Social Security retirement eligibility, mostly due to begin in the next century, will ratchet up the retirement age. This is to account for the already-present, coincidental approach to retirement age of the Post-World War II baby boomers and the relative shortage of young workers to replace and support them.

Drugs and AIDS will probably continue as plagues through the next decade.

Poverty and homelessness will also continue. Poverty, once a problem of the elderly, has changed; 40 percent of the poor in 1988 were children. Homelessness, once a problem of detached, adult males, became a family problem in the 1980s. Low- and middle-income housing declined. Those trends may continue.

Science and technology will continue to fuel the communications and information revolutions and facilitate further paradigm shifts in health services and behavioral sciences. Fewer jobs will be created for the marginally literate. The gap will widen between the educationally advantaged and the marginally skilled.

Political and governmental changes Two broad, national political trends since the late 1960s were identified earlier: partisan politicization and deinstitutionalization. This is an era of New Spoils, dominated by the executive, but enthusiastically shared by many legislators, feeding on large government and financing costly, media-dominated elections and related political operations.

A precursor to these developments was something of a paradigm shift that occurred in much of political science during the 1950s and 1960s. That change was driven by the new technologies of opinion polling, elections analysis, and media campaigning. Old philosophical outlooks were largely shunted aside, along with traditional concerns about constitutional values, disciplines, and institutions. Power became the purpose of politics; authority was displaced as a political foundation; legitimacy, determined by politics, became the final test of power. And the new technologies were quickly put to work to manipulate public opinion to win elections and power. Presidential primaries and the general election in 1988 illustrated that this development is growing, not abating.

Executive aggrandizement was noted earlier as a tenet of public administration that was elevated to orthodoxy during the Structural Discipline Period of council-manager government. That orthodoxy dominated the entire field, not simply local government. The doctrine took a crucial turn during the 1970s and 1980s, particularly at the national level. Responsibility of employees of the executive branch—public servants—had generally been first to the law and then to authoritative missions before the 1970s. Expectations of first loyalty then shifted; loyalty to the President became the expectation in a system that turned away from traditional practices of shared constitutional powers to a conflict-oriented concept of separation of powers. This outlook also increasingly characterizes state governments and many mayor-council jurisdictions. In short, it is the growing climate of transactional American politics.

Council-manager government is increasingly pressured by these two interrelated political paradigms: *legitimacy of power and loyalty to the powerful.*

Besides council-manager government, other forces support continued efforts to sustain alternative values of constitutional institutions and popular self-governance. Many political leaders at national, state, and local levels support traditional values of non-self-serving civic duty. The National Commission on the Public Service (the Volcker Commission) in 1988–1989 was one of several organized efforts to restore transformational values to government, for example. By 1988, the National Academy of Public Administration (NAPA), while continuing to support extensive executive power, had turned increasingly toward the shared-powers concept of the Constitution, and NAPA supported first loyalty to the law in its 1988 transition report, *The Executive Presidency: Federal Management for the 1990s.*[9]

Future challenges   The greatest challenge for council-manager governments in the United States during the decade of the 1990s is to help restore to the nation the transformational disciplines of constitutional democracy: civic duty and public service in support of human dignity and a rule of law. They can do this in part by focusing on "The Essential Community," as urged by ICMA's Future Horizons Committee.

Writing in 1979 and 1980, that group expected the challenges to be difficult in the 1980s and to become easier in the 1990s. They did not foresee the creation of a national debt that, by the 1990s, may require nearly 15 percent of the annual budget of the United States to service. They did not anticipate an AIDS plague that is expected to consume extensive resources in the 1990s. They did not expect low- and moderate-income housing to dwindle as disastrously as it did in the 1980s. Other developments sketched above were largely foreseen in the 1970s by ICMA professionals and their associates.

Because of the national debt and incapacities of the United States government, local governments must deal with many of these problems without much help. In a new sense, local governments are the hope of essential community not only at the important level of neighborhoods, as projected in the 1970s, but nationally as well.

Council-manager government remains as the strongest institutional force of transformational politics in practice in the United States. Its basic tenet of collaborative, community-oriented politics, combined with the qualities of disciplined institutions and professionally responsible expertise, stand in contrast to more visible trends in national politics and government.

Which political forces, transactional or transformational, will prosper in the 1990s remains an open question. Only the seriousness of the answer is clear. That is a high challenge worthy of the transformational idealism of council-manager government. It is a challenge that demonstrates again a lesson of long experience: in constitutional democracy, realism requires the disciplined practice of ideals.

1. ICMA Committee on Future Horizons, ... *New Worlds of Service* (Washington D.C.: ICMA, 1979).
2. Laurence Rutter, *The Essential Community: Local Government in the Year 2000* (Washington D.C.: ICMA, 1980).
3. ICMA Committee, *New Worlds*, cover page.
4. Keith F. Mulrooney, "The American City Manager: An Urban Administrator in a Complex and Evolving Situation," *Public Administration Review* 31 (January/February 1971): 2–46.
5. Aaron Wildavsky, "Ubiquitous Anomie: Public Service in an Era of Ideological Dissensus," *Public Administration Review* 48 (July/August 1988): 753–755; Robert B. Denhardt and Edward T. Jennings, "Image and Integrity in the Public Service," *Public Administration Review* 49 (January/February 1989): 74–77; Aaron Wildavsky, "Ubiquitous Anomie: Reflections and Rejoinder," *Public Administration Review* 49 (January/February 1989): 74–77.

6. ICMA Committee, *New Worlds*, 1.
7. Elizabeth K. Kellar, "Future Horizons: Then and Now," *Public Management* 70 (April 1988): 14–15.
8. Numerous publications provide insights on future trends. Sources used in this section include: Special Committee on Aging, United States Senate, *America in Transition: An Aging Society*, Serial No. 99-B (Washington D.C.: U.S. Government Printing Office, June 1985); William B. Johnston and Arnold E. Packer, *Workforce 2000* (Indianapolis: Hudson Institute, June 1987); John F. W. Rogers *et al.*, *Meeting Public Demands: Federal Services in the Year 2000* (Washington, D.C.: U.S. Government Printing Office, January 1988).
9. Elmer B. Staats *et al.*, *The Executive Presidency: Federal Management for the 1990s* (Washington, D.C.: National Academy of Public Administration, September 1988).

Politics for a Troubled Planet

———————————— Frances Moore Lappé

Laments about political apathy among Americans are about as common as surfers on a Santa Barbara beach in June. The near-record low voter turnout in the last election fed these laments. But it is not simply apathy many Americans feel: it is anger. Americans are insulted by our political process. During the last presidential race, the daily news story was not the candidates' latest position on critical issues, but analysis of how the candidate's managers were manipulating us that day. No wonder people feel uneasy.

And no wonder so many feel disconnected from a system that treats them as simple objects, not citizens. Youth polled recently by Peter D. Hart for People for the American Way said that they do not see a connection between their concerns about questions like "homeless people walking the streets" or "kids selling drugs" and government policies—either as causes or solutions. Thus, the young people polled "do not see political participation as a way to address the problems," Hart concluded.

Reinforcing their feelings of distance from politics, many young people have a negative, even cartoon-like image of politicians, according to the poll. Words like "dishonest," "corrupt," and "liars" were commonly used descriptions.

Youth's conception of citizenship was notably passive. When asked if they are good citizens, the participants reported that they are because "they don't do anything wrong," or "don't do anything to hurt anybody else." Citizenship meant simply avoiding trouble, not taking active responsibility.

But if Americans don't see a connection between their concerns and what is understood as "politics," it does not mean that we are not active in our communities. Roughly half of all adult Americans volunteer in a variety of causes, giving an average of almost five hours a week. Three-fourths of us contribute an average of almost $800 a year to charities of all types.

So, what then is the problem? Why do our political institutions appear unable to reverse the downward slide we feel ourselves on? Why don't Americans perceive the political process as a vehicle for expressing their anger, their concerns and their values?

Project Public Life

Our work is based upon a simple hypothesis: only through democratic renewal can we as a people begin to conceive of meeting the threats to our society and our planet. Precisely because of the scale and complexity of today's problems, they cannot be solved outside of a social process of growing citizen knowledge and responsibility: what I call *citizen democracy*.

There is no way to short circuit the renewal of democratic politics—the reshaping of ourselves in relation to one another in a public world—if we are to seriously address the problems we face. But as *Washington Post* columnist Colman McCarthy has recently reminded us, "the trouble with all good ideas is that they soon degenerate into hard work." So I offer some thoughts on that hard work needed to build citizen democracy.

Harry C. Boyte of the Humphrey Institute at the University of Minnesota and I have convened a national partnership this year on the theme of political renewal, reaching out to include associations and groups as varied as YMCAs, libraries, 4-H Clubs, youth service organizations, community colleges, public interest groups, and nonpartisan community organizations like those associated with the Industrial Areas Foundation. We call it Project Public Life. Our goal is to help reformulate the discussion about what "politics" means in America, in large part through projects that enhance citizen capacity for public judgment and public agency. We call this learning the "political arts," incorporating the skilled use of power, imagination, judgment, listening, and reflection on experience.

Our project seeks especially to help existing organizations founded with the purpose of enhancing active citizenship to revitalize their public mission. An obvious place to begin is where people are already engaged in discussion of civic life. The classroom is one. So, my most recent book, *Rediscovering America's Values*, was written as a dialogue about the founding principles of our society—democracy, freedom and fairness—in part precisely to stir up such classroom discourse. Our goal is to transform dull, detached courses in government, political science and philosophy—courses now reinforcing a sense of politics as a spectator sport—into charged, interactive sessions. Here, young people can be challenged to grapple with their own values and life's purposes and begin to learn the skills for effective public life.

We expect to expand such classroom discussion projects into a larger effort, through study circles and other forums that combine community discussions around issues with deliberation on what citizens actually can do about key public problems. In so doing, we begin to deepen what Daniel Yankelovich has called "public judgment," or the informed, many-sided perspective that emerges when people learn to listen to each other. Public judgment differs sharply from mere public opinion: the unreflected views of private individuals.

Another example of our project is a collaborative effort to develop for public interest organizations a form of constituency education with strong reflective and conceptual dimensions. A large public interest network of organizations has developed over the past two decades, especially through the use of "one-directional" communication technologies like direct mail and door-to-door canvassing. But to build strong and active memberships in these groups will require different forms of constituency education: leadership-training programs that help members think through questions such as power, judgment, the nature of public life, the need for an artful practice of reflection on particular campaigns, and the importance of celebration, ritual and recognition in organizational development. We expect to undertake this in partnership with the Advocacy Institute of Washington, D.C.

A third part of the project will help create "new commons"— meeting grounds in communities, housed in places like the local library—where citizens gain access to useful civic information materials, and reestablish practices of face-to-face discussion of community concerns. We anticipate working with the ACCESS Network in the Public Interest and others on this project.

In all these kinds of efforts, we want to stress a caveat: Democratic renewal presumes that our viability as a healthy and fair society depends upon our capacity to transcend the ethos of radical individualism, so far out of synch with today's realities. But we must be careful to remember that such a path does *not* mean remaking human nature. Throughout modern history those seeking social change have turned their ideals to totalitarian impositions when seeking the reconstruction of the person (e.g., the perversions involved in the idea of the "new socialist man"). We reject such views. Instead, we are building on forgotten traits which a variety of thoughtful observers have pointed to in human psychology.

Conclusion: Three forgotten traits

Connectedness   First is an innate sense of connectedness to each other's well-being. Here we need to remember old wisdom. Even Charles Darwin, whose theories were for so long misused to defend dog-eat-dog morality, clearly believed that evolving human beings could only have sustained and expanded our societies because of a "moral sense . . . aboriginally derived from the social instincts." Among primeval people, Darwin observed, actions were no doubt judged good or bad "solely as they obviously affect the welfare of the tribe." Similarly, Adam Smith, so long identified with the greed principle of human motivation, in fact argued that human beings are profoundly interdependent. In *The Theory of Moral Sentiments*, he wrote that "[man] is sensible that his own interest is connected with the prosperity of society, and that the happiness, perhaps the preservation, of his existence, depends upon its preservation."

Such a view, moreover, is increasingly confirmed by comparative sociology, anthropology and psychology. Recent studies find the roots of empathy in infancy, noting that infants react to the pain of others as though they were feeling it themselves. Thus, the challenge is not to create "social instincts," as Darwin called them; rather, it is to ask how we have denied them and how we might call them forth, now that they are crucial to our world.

Purpose   Second, a public-minded approach to the future assumes a human need for purpose. Psychologists now confirm that most people have a greater sense of well being when they contribute time or money to something they care about beyond themselves. In fact, many psychologists argue that our mental health depends on it.

Creativity   Third and finally, an approach based on the possibility of democratic social change assumes that human beings are not only capable of understanding our interdependency, are not only creatures in need of purpose, but also that we are *creative* beings. Here, above all, we can turn to our society's roots. Our nation was founded on the belief that, indeed, something new is possible under the sun. At the time, many considered the principles of the Declaration of Independence to be utter madness! James Madison, when near death, said that America proved what before was believed impossible. And Thomas Jefferson believed that people are capable of infinite creativity. He wrote that "laws and institutions must go hand in hand with the progress of the human mind." Our very birthright is the capacity to envision and create a future.

Regenerating Community

—————————————— John L. McKnight

Each of us has a map of the social world in our mind. The way we act, our plans, and opinions are the result of that map.

The people who make social policy also have social maps in their minds. They make plans and design programs based on their map. Indeed, if you carefully examine their programs, you can detect the nature of their mental map.

Using this method, we have found that the most common social policy map has two locations: institutions and individual people. By institutions we mean large structures such as corporations, universities, and government mental health systems. These structures organize a large group of people so that a few of them will be able to control the rest of them. In this structure, there is ultimately room for one leader. It is a structure initially created to produce goods such as steel and automobiles.

In the last few decades, the structure has also been used to design human service systems. While these newly designed, hierarchical, managed service systems do not produce goods such as steel, they do produce needs assessments, service plans, protocols, and procedures. They are also thought, by some policymakers, to produce health, education, security, or justice.

If it is correct that these systems can produce these service commodities, then it is possible to imagine that there are consumers of their products. For example, we have all heard that there are now people called "health consumers." They are the individuals who are the other part of the social map created by most social policymakers. They make a complete economic world by acting as the users

Reprinted with permission from the *Kettering Review*, Fall 1989.

(consumers) of the products of managed institutional producers of such commodities as mental health, health, education, and justice. Thus, we can see that it was necessary to create health consumers once we had systems that could produce health. Otherwise, there would be no purpose for these large, hierarchical, managed systems.

Once we understand this social map of institutions and individuals we can see why we have mental health providers and mental health consumers. We can also see how our developing service economy works.

Because the Gross National Product is the sum of the goods and services produced each year, many policy experts have come to believe that the well-being of our society significantly depends upon the amount of the commodities called services that are produced by institutions and used by consumers. For example, a person with a perilous and extended illness (a health consumer) contributes significantly to our economic growth by using large amounts of the commodities produced by the "health system." Indeed, a very ill person disabled for a considerable amount of time could cause production of much more medical dollar value through his illness than the value of his own production as, say, a healthy florist.

This amazing development is possible, in part, because of the unusual two-place map used by many social policymakers in designing social service programs. Unfortunately, this map and the program designs that flow from it have recently encountered three major problems.

Recalcitrant consumers

The first problem is that in spite of ever-growing inputs into institutionalized service systems, many individuals continue to reject their roles as consumers. This is the problem of intractability that has resulted in an increasing focus upon the "compliance" issue. Especially in our big cities, many intractable young individuals continue to refuse to learn in spite of heightened resources and managerial inputs to school systems. This is commonly known as the educational problem.

Similarly, there are many other intractable individuals who refuse to behave in spite of our correctional institutions. This is the crime problem.

There is also the nutrition problem created by intractable people who refuse to eat the right food. And the chemical dependency problem created by intractable people who insist on smoking and drinking incorrectly. There is also the ever-growing number of intractable people who refuse to flourish in institutions created for labeled people, in spite of all the professional and managerial improvements designed by the systems.

Indeed, there are so many intractable people refusing to consume institutional services that we are now designing new systems that surround these individuals with professionally administered services. Thus, one can now see individuals whose lives are bounded by institutions "targeting" their services at an intractable individual through such professionals as teachers, doctors, trainers, social workers, family planners, psychologists, vocational counselors, and security officers. This final solution is usually called a "comprehensive, multidisciplinary, coordinated, interagency service system." It is the equivalent of institutionalization without walls or the design of an environment to create a totally dependent service system consumer.

The bottomless pit

The second problem with programs based upon the typical social policy map is that the sum of their costs can be greater than the wealth of the nation. In a recent white paper entitled "A Time to Serve" (Pergamon Press), a group of Swedish government planners described the escalating costs of their much-acclaimed social service system. They point out that at present rates of growth, the system could consume the entire nation's wealth within a few decades. Therefore, they propose that the government begin to "tax" people's time by requiring the Swedish people to contribute unpaid work to the maintenance and growth of their social service system.

While it is clearly the case that the United States is not in immediate danger of the Swedish economic dilemma, we are contributing substantial amounts to social service systems. A recent study by the Community Services Society of New York found that approximately $7,000 per capita of public and private money is specifically allocated to the low-income population of that city. Thus, a family of four would be eligible on a per capita basis for $28,000 which would place them in the moderate income category. However, only 37 percent of this money actually reaches low-income people in income. Nearly two-thirds is consumed by those who service the poor.

The third problem with the typical social policy map is that programs based on its suppositions are increasingly ineffective and even counterproductive. For example, we now understand that our "correctional systems" consistently train people in crime. Studies demonstrate that a substantial number of people, while in hospitals, become sick or injured with maladies worse than those for which they were admitted. In many of our big city schools we see children whose relative achievement levels fall farther behind each year. Thus, we have come to recognize the possibility that we can create crime-making corrections systems, sickness-making health systems, and stupid-making schools based upon a social model that conceives society as a place bounded by institutions and individuals.

It is obvious upon the briefest reflection that the typical social policy map is inaccurate because it excludes a major social do-main—the community. By community, we mean the social place used by family, friends, neighbors, neighborhood associations, clubs, civic groups, local enterprises, churches, ethnic associations, tem-ples, local unions, local government, and local media. In addition to being called the community, this social environment is also de-scribed as the informal sector, the unmanaged environment, and the associational sector.

The communal alternative

These associations of community represent unique social tools that are unlike the social tool represented by a managed institution. For example, the structure of institutions is a design established to cre-ate control of people. On the other hand, the structure of associa-tions is the result of people acting through consent. It is critical that we distinguish between these two motive forces because there are many goals that can only be fulfilled through consent, and these are often goals that will be impossible to achieve through a production system designed to control.

There are many other unique characteristics of the community of associations:

The associations in community are *interdependent*. To weaken one is to weaken all. If the local newspaper closes, the garden club and the township meeting will each diminish as they lose a voice. If the American Legion disbands, several community fund-raising events and the maintenance of the ballpark will stop. If the Baptist Church closes, several self-help groups that meet in the basement will be without a home and folks in the old people's home will lose their weekly visitors. The interdependence of associations and the dependence of community upon their work is the vital center of an effective society.

The community environment is constructed around the recog-nition of fallibility rather than the ideal. Most institutions, on the other hand, are designed with a vision imagining a structure where things can be done right, a kind of orderly perfection achieved, and the ablest dominate. In contrast, community structures tend to pro-liferate until they create a place for everyone, no matter how falli-ble. They provide vehicles that give voice to diversity and assume that consensual contribution is the primary value. In this prolifera-tion of community associations, there is room for many leaders and the development of leadership capacity among many. This demo-cratic opportunity structure assumes that the best idea is the sum of the knowings of the collected fallible people who are citizens. In-deed, it is the marvel of the democratic ideal that people of every fallibility are citizens. Effective associational life incorporates all of those fallibilities and reveals the unique intelligence of community.

Swift and flexible　Associations have the *capacity to respond quickly*. They do not need to involve all of the institutional interests incorporated in such agencies as a planning committee, budget, office, and administrative staff. A primary characteristic of people who need help is that their problem is created by the unexpected tragedy, the surprise development, the sudden change. While they will be able to stabilize over the long run, what they often need is immediate help. The rapid response capacity of associations, and their interconnectedness, allows for the possibility of immediate and comprehensive assistance without first initiating a person into a system from which they may never leave.

The proliferation and development of community associations allows for the flowering of creative solutions. Institutions tend to require creative ideas to follow channels. However, the nonhierarchical nature of the field of associations allows us to see all of the budding ideas and greatly increases our opportunities for the flowering of social innovation.

Because community associations are small, face-to-face groups, the relationship among members is very individualized. They also have the tradition of dealing with nonmembers as individuals. Institutions, on the other hand, have great difficulty developing programs or activities that recognize the unique characteristics of each individual. Therefore, associations represent unusual tools for creating hand-tailored responses to those who may be in special need or have unique fallibilities.

Our institutions are constantly reforming and reorganizing themselves in an effort to create or allow relationships that can be characterized as "care." Nonetheless, their ministrations consistently turn themselves into commodities and become services. For many people with uncommon fallibilities, their need is for care rather than service. While a managed system organized as a structure of control can deliver a service, it cannot deliver care. Care is a special relationship characterized by consent rather than control. Therefore, its auspices are individual and associational. For those who need care, we must recognize the community as the appropriate social tool.

Participatory democracy　Finally, associations and the community they create are the forum within which citizenship can be expressed. Institutions by their managed structure are definitionally unable to act as forums for citizenship. Therefore, the vital center of democracy is the community of associations. Any person without access to that forum is effectively denied citizenship. For those people with unique fallibilities who have been institutionalized, it isn't enough that they be deinstitutionalized. In order to be a citizen, they must also have the opportunity for recommunalization.

In summary, the community of associations provides a social tool where consent is the primary motivation, interdependence creates holistic environments, people of all capacities and fallibilities are incorporated, quick responses are possible, creativity is multiplied rather than channeled, individualized responses are characteristic, care is able to replace service, and citizenship is possible. When all of these unique capacities of community are recognized, it is obvious why the social policy map that excludes community life has resulted in increasing failures. To exclude from our problem-solving capacities the social tool of community is to have taken the heart out of America.

Three visions

Why is it, then, that social policy maps so often ignore such an important continent as community? One reason is that there are many institutional leaders who simply do not believe in the capacities of communities. They often see communities as collections of parochial, inexpert, uninformed, and biased people. Indeed, there are many leaders of service systems who believe that they are in direct competition with communities for the power to correctly define problems, provide scientific solutions and professional services.

In this competitive understanding, the institutional leaders are correct. Whenever hierarchical systems become more powerful than the community, we see the flow of authority, resources, skills, dollars, legitimacy, and capacities away from communities to service systems. In fact, institutionalized systems grow at the expense of communities. As institutions gain power, communities lose their potency and the consent of community is replaced by the control of systems; the care of community is replaced by the service of systems; the citizens of community are replaced by the clients and consumers of institutional products.

Today our society is the site of the struggle between community and institution for the capacities and loyalties of our people. This struggle is never carried out in the abstract. Instead, it occurs each day in the relations of people, the budget decisions of systems, and the public portraits of the media. As one observes this struggle, there appear to be three visions of society that dominate the discourse.

The first is the Therapeutic Vision. This prospect sees the well-being of individuals as growing from an environment composed of professionals and their services. It envisions a world where there is a professional to meet every need, and the fee to secure each professional service is a right. This vision is epigrammatically expressed by those who see the ultimate liberty as "the right to treatment."

The second prospect is the Advocacy Vision. This approach foresees a world in which labeled people will be in an environment protected by advocates and advocacy groups. It conceives an individual whose world is guarded by legal advocates, support people, self-help groups, job developers, and housing locaters. Unlike the therapeutic vision, the advocacy approach conceives a defensive wall of helpers to protect an individual against an alien community. It seeks to ensure a person's right to be a functioning individual.

The third approach is the Community Vision. It sees the goal as recommunalization of exiled and labeled individuals. It understands the community as the basic context for enabling people to contribute their gifts. It sees community associations as contexts to create and locate jobs, provide opportunities for recreation and multiple friendships, and to become the political defender of the right of labeled people to be free from exile.

Those who seek to institute the community vision believe that beyond therapy and advocacy is the constellation of community associations—the church, the bowling league, the garden club, the town paper, the American Legion, the hardware store, and the township board. They see a society where those who were once labeled, exiled, treated, counseled, advised, and protected are instead incorporated in community where their contributions, capacities, gifts, and fallibilities will allow a network of relationships involving work, recreation, friendship, support, and the political power of being a citizen.

Qualities of community

Because so many labeled people have been exiled to a world expressing the professional and advocacy vision of an appropriate life, the community vision has frequently been forgotten. How will people know when they are in community? Our studies suggest that this universe is distinctive and distinguished from the environment of systems and institutions. The community experience incorporates:

Capacity   We all remember the childhood question regarding how to describe a glass with water to its midpoint: is it half full or half empty? Community associations are built upon the recognition of the fullness of each member because it is the sum of their capacities that represents the power of the group. The social policy mapmakers, on the other hand, build a world based on the emptiness of each of us—a model based upon deficiency. Communities depend on capacities. Systems make commodities of deficiencies.

Collective effort   It is obvious that the essence of community is people working together. One of the characteristics of this community work is shared responsibility that requires many talents. Thus, a person who has been labeled deficient can find a hammock of support in the collective capacities of a community that can shape itself to the unique character of each person. This collective process contrasts with the individualistic approach of the therapeutic professional and the rigidity of institutions that demand that people shape themselves to the needs of the system.

Informality   Associational life in the community is a critical element of the informal economy. Here transactions of value take place without money, advertising, or hype. Authentic relationships are possible, and care emerges in place of its packaged imitation—service.

The informality of community is also expressed through relationships that are not managed. Communities viewed by those who only understand managed experiences and relationships appear to be disordered, messy, and inefficient. What these people fail to understand is that there is a hidden order to community groups that is determined by the need to incorporate capacity and fallibility.

While institutions and professionals war against human fallibility by trying to replace it, cure it, or disregard it, communities are proliferations of associations that multiply until they incorporate both the capacities and the fallibilities of citizens. It is for this reason that labeled people are not out of place in community, because they all have capacities and only their fallibilities are unusual. However, because there are so many community associations, there are always some sets of associational relationships that can incorporate their fallibilities and use their unique gifts.

Stories   In universities, people know through studies. In businesses and bureaucracies, people know by reports. In communities, people know by stories. These community stories allow people to reach back into their common history and their individual experience for knowledge about truth and direction for the future.

Professionals and institutions often threaten the stories of community by urging community people to count up things rather than communicate. Successful community associations resist efforts to impose the foreign language of studies and reports because it is a tongue that ignores their own capacities and insights. Whenever communities come to believe that their common knowledge is illegitimate, they lose their power and professionals and systems rapidly invade their social place.

Celebration   Community groups constantly incorporate celebrations, parties, and social events in their activities. The line between work and play is blurred and the human nature of everyday life becomes part of the way of work. You will know that you are in community if you often hear laughter and singing. You will know you are in an institution, corporation, or bureaucracy if you hear the silence of long halls and reasoned meetings. Associations in community celebrate because they work by consent and have the luxury of allowing joyfulness to join them in their endeavors.

Tragedy The surest indication of the experience of community is the explicit common knowledge of tragedy, death, and suffering. The managed, ordered, technical vision embodied in professional and institutional systems leaves no space for tragedy. They are basically methods for production and have no room for tragedy. Indeed, they are designed to deny the central dilemmas of life. Therefore, our managed systems gladly give communities the real dilemmas of the human condition. There is no competition here. Therefore, to be in community is to be an active part of the consolation of associations and self-help groups. To be in community is to be a part of ritual, lamentation, and celebration of our fallibility.

Citizenship redeemed

Knowing community is not an abstract understanding. Rather, it is what we each know about all of us.

As we think about ourselves, our community and institutions, many of us recognize that we have been degraded because our roles as citizens and our communities have been traded in for the right to "clienthood" and consumer status. Many of us have come to recognize that as we exiled our fallible neighbors to the control of managers, therapists, and technicians, we lost much of our power to be the vital center of society. We forgot about the capacity of every single one of us to do good work and, instead, made some of us into the objects of good works—servants of those who serve.

As we think about our community life, we recognize that something has happened to many of us as institutions have grown in power: we have become too impotent to be called real citizens and too disconnected to be effective members of community.

There is a mistaken notion that our society has a problem in terms of effective human services. Our essential problem is weak communities. While we have reached the limits of institutional problem solving, we are only at the beginning of exploring the possibility of a new vision for community. It is a vision of regeneration. It is a vision of reassociating the exiled. It is a vision of freeing ourselves from service and advocacy. It is a vision of centering our lives in community.

We all know that community must be the center of our life because it is only in community that we can be citizens. It is only in community that we can find care. It is only in community that we can hear people singing. And if you listen carefully, you can hear the words:

I care for you,
because you are mine,
and I am yours.

For Further Reference

Agor, Weston H. "Intuition and Strategic Planning." *The Futurist* (November-December 1989): 20-23.

Cappo, Joe. *FutureScope: Success Strategies for the 1990s and Beyond.* Chicago: Longman Financial Services Publishing, 1990.

Carlyle, Ralph. "The Tomorrow Organization." *Datamation* (February 1, 1990): 22-29.

Center, John. "Where America Was a Century Ago: History as a Guide to the Future." *The Futurist* (January-February 1990): 22-28.

Cetron, Marvin, and Owen Davies. *American Renaissance: Our Life at the Turn of the 21st Century.* New York: St. Martin's Press, 1989.

Cetron, Marvin, and Owen Davies. "Future Trends." *Omni* (October 1989): 114-118.

Clark, Kim B. "What Strategy Can Do for Technology." *Harvard Business Review* (November-December 1989): 94-98.

Conner, Roger L. "Answering the Demo-Doomsayers." *The Brookings Review* (Fall 1989): 35-39.

Cornish, Edward. "Issues of the '90s." *The Futurist* (January-February 1990): 29-36.

Cronis, Thomas E. *Direct Democracy: The Politics of Initiative, Referendum, and Recall.* Cambridge, MA: Harvard University Press, 1989.

Didsbury, Howard F., Jr., ed. *The Future: Opportunity, Not Destiny.* Bethesda, MD: World Future Society, 1989.

Drucker, Peter. *The New Realities.* New York: Harper and Row, 1989.

Inayatullah, Sohail. "Sarkar's Spiritual Dialectics: An Unconventional View of the Future." *Futures* (February 1988): 54-65.

Long, Marion. "City Scripts." *Omni* (October 1989): 50; 126-133.

Main, Jeremy. "The Winning Organization." *Fortune* (September 26, 1988): 50-60.

Nulty, Peter. "How the World Will Change." *Fortune* (January 15, 1990): 44-54.

Pelton, Joseph N. "Telepower: The Emerging Global Brain." *The*

Futurist (September-October 1989): 9–14.

Robins, Kevin, and Mark Hepworth. "Electronic Spaces: New Technologies and the Future of Cities." *Futures* (April 1988): 155–176.

Rush, Howard, and Ian Miles. "Surveying the Social Implications of Information Technology." *Futures* (June 1989): 249–262.

"Special Supplement on Education." *The Wall Street Journal* (February 9, 1990): R1–R36.

Starr, Douglas. "Brainstorms: The World's Top Think Tanks Predict the Future." *Omni* (October 1989): 67–135.

World Future Society. The World Future Society is an excellent resource for publications, videos, and software dealing with a wide variety of futures issues. World Future Society, 4916 Saint Elmo Avenue, Bethesda, MD 20814.

Practical Management Series

Managing for Tomorrow: Global Change and Local Futures

Text type
Century Expanded

Composition
Applied Graphics Technologies
Washington, D.C.

Printing and binding
R. R. Donnelley & Sons Company
Harrisonburg, Virginia

Cover design
Rebecca Geanaros